UNSHAKEABLE MARRIAGE

A Biblical Blueprint for Strong Relationships

by

ROBERT L. SCHECK

Hallelujah Ministries International

Foreword By

DR. MYLES MUNROE

All Scripture quotations are taken from the *Holy Bible*, New King James Version, copyright © 1979, 1980, 1982. Used by permission of Thomas Nelson, Inc., Nashville, Tennessee.

Unshakeable Marriage: A Biblical Blueprint for Strong Relationships

ISBN: 0-924748-61-3
UPC: 88571300031-4

Printed in the United States of America
© 2005 by Robert L. Scheck

Milestones International Publishers
4410 University Dr., Ste. 113
Huntsville, AL 35816
(256) 536-9402, ext. 234; Fax: (256) 536-4530
www.milestonesintl.com

1 2 3 4 5 6 7 8 9 10 11 / 09 08 07 06 05

Endorsements

❧❀❧

God's covenants are the foundation of our faith. They establish the promises and ground rules for our relationship with Him. Pastor Robert Scheck has laid them out with clarity in a way that will help you understand the elements of the covenants, how we have violated them, the consequences, and how to be restored to the covenant relationship with God that He designed and desires. Pastor Scheck's transparency in relating his own journey will encourage you and change your life!

Dr. Lawrence Kennedy
Senior Pastor, North Church—Dallas, TX
Bishop/President, Church on the Rock International

Pastor Robert Scheck is a member of Church on the Rock International. We know him to be a man of integrity and a pure heart. They shine through in this book. The wonderful message is that, even though we have failed to uphold our end of the covenants God has established with us, He knew that we would fail so, He Himself took our place—and our consequences—on our behalf. He is our Covenant Keeper and Redeemer from death. This book will make you realize anew the debt we owed and the grace we have received!

Dr. Eddie Mitchell
Executive Director, Church on the Rock International

"*Unshakable Marriage* (formerly *Returning to Eden*) is overflowing with fresh revelation. Pastor Robert teaches us in this wonderful book how sacred our marriages are to the Lord. Using covenant principles, this book simplifies all of our relationship questions. This book is a must read."

Dr. Jeffrey S. Burnett
Assistant Professor
Wellness Center Coordinator
Health and Human Performance
Fort Hays State University

More than just another book on relationships, *Unshakable Marriage* gives solid instruction to couples as they navigate the sometimes turbulent waters of marriage. Both your marriage and your life will be blessed as you read and study this book.

Dr. James B. Richards
Best-selling Author, *Breaking the Cycle* and
How to Stop the Pain

Life is based on relationships. Robert and I met many years ago through a divine connection. Through these many years our relationship has gotten stronger. And of course, we have both gotten smarter.

In his book, *Unshakable Marriage* (formerly *Returning to Eden*), Robert brings out the covenants that have been given to man, ending with the most important: Jesus Christ, The New Covenant. You will find that when God created mankind, He did not want an army. He had angels for that. He wanted a family, a family with whom to have friendship, fellowship and love. Robert brings out all this when he teaches on having a strong marriage relationship based on God's love.

I know you will be encouraged as you read and study the covenant principles that Robert has given to you in this wonderful book.

Dr. Dave Duell, Founder
Faith Ministries International Network and
Faith Ministries Church International
Denver, Colorado USA

Reflecting back to our first time meeting in 1998, I realize today how much our steps were divinely ordered by the Lord. I thank God for linking you with The International Third World Leaders Association under the leadership of Dr. Myles Munroe, chairman. Your presence at our Global Leadership Summits has always been an enhancement to the meetings. It is without a doubt, that you were suppose to be in Dr. Myles Munroe's sphere of relationships, because your purpose is linked to his vision to "Promote

Change Through Leadership." As I reflect upon the work that you have put into print, I believe this is only the beginning of where God is about to launch you internationally. The world has yet to discover who Robert L. Sheck is and when that happens, millions will realize it ocurred through the renewing of their minds through your *Unshakable Marriage* (formerly *Returning to Eden*) book. Congratulations and dare to keep dreaming! You are on the right road in pursuit of your destiny.

Lucile Richardson, Ed.D.
Provost/International Leadership Training Institute
Nassau, Bahamas

About the Cover

⟨ornament⟩

Robert wrote this poem to Jill as a wedding present.

You and I

Some ask—Where are we going?

Why do we pass the time away?

What are these strange happenings

that fill our night and day?

Why am I here and why also must you be?

What is the meaning of this short life

and all the things I see?

Who is God?—What is Love?

Questions asked by every man.

Each with his own concept

he tries to understand.

This is our quest, though sometimes

futile it may seem.

But come, take my hand.

We two can find this dream.

We will grow more at each sunset

and walk along the sea.

And make sense of just what life is

and what you mean to me.

And when all this is over,

and there's nothing left but sky,

We will share the answers forever

Together—you and I.

R.L.SCHECK

Table of Contents

1000-Fold Partners

***

- Ron & Cindy Barker, "Covenant Partners," Elizabeth, Colorado

- Bob & Susan Buergisser, Arvada Colorado

- Mel & Cathy Coleman, Broomfield Colorado

- Kirk & Treva Johnston, Hays, Kansas

- Jeremy Reynolds, Hays, Kansas

- Marvin Simoneau, Lafayette, Colorado

- John & Becky Sparks, "Trinity Builders," Greenville, Texas

- Raul & Margarita Torrez, "Mannatech," Thornton, Colorado

- Marshall (Butch) & Ann Warren, "Freedom Reins," Loveland, Colorado

Acknowledgments

We dedicate this labor of love to Our Heavenly Father, Our Lord and Savior, Jesus Christ, and to the Holy Spirit, without whose ministry and inspiration this book would not have been possible.

We would also like to express our deepest gratitude to all the people who have prayed for us, and especially to all the teachers and pastors who have patiently and lovingly labored, mentored, and discipled us.

Thank you Lord, for our wonderful parents!

Special recognition goes to Richard and Vi Vigil for their unending support of this ministry. Thank You, Lord, for blessing them as they have blessed us.

Finally, we would like to acknowledge in particular the ministries of the following:

Pastor Craig Hill, Family Foundations International, Littleton, Colorado

The late Dr.Fuchsia Pickett, in Heaven

Dr. Myles Munroe, Bahama Faith Ministries, Nassau Bahamas

Sincerely, in His service,

Robert L. Scheck, author
Jill Vigil Scheck, editor
Pastors, Hallelujah Ministries International.

Foreword

The crisis of family disintegration, marital collapse and broken relationships is a global epidemic that impacts everybody's life in some way today. No culture, society or social class is immune. The need for help in the restoration of the family structure and strong homes is the focus of governments, social scientists, and the man on the street. This can be done if we are willing to return to the sound foundations of the Creator of the human family, and follow His time-tested instructions.

In *Unshakable Marriage* (formerly *Returning to Eden*), Robert Scheck provides practical, time-tested principles to help us recapture the purpose for marriage relationships and family. In his crisp, provocative style he simplifies the complex, making it easy to understand the nature of relationships. I challenge you to read this book and keep it as a companion to your life. It has the tools you need to strengthen your marriage, heal the hurts, and destroy the confusion that comes with living in a world without meaning. Let this book help you discover the true purpose, design and plan God has for your life and family. Start today to build the strong, unshakeable relationship you have always dreamed of.

Dr. Myles Munroe
Nassau, Bahamas

Preface

※⚘⚘⚘※

Then God said, "Let us make man in Our image, according to Our likeness; let them have domin- ion...over all the earth..." (Genesis. 1:26).

This is how it all began, but why? Why did God cre- ate man? What was God's original intent and pur- pose? What was in it for Him? What was in it for us? What is the meaning of life? Who am I and why am I here? Why are any of us here? Where are we going and what are we supposed to be doing along the way? Is this life as we perceive it all there is? If not, what comes next?

These questions have haunted the heart of man throughout human history. People of every culture and every generation have pondered the puzzle of human exis- tence, but few have ever found a truly satisfactory solu- tion. The purpose of this present study is to offer biblical answers to these questions as I believe they have been revealed by the Holy Spirit of God. I make no claim to possess all the answers but simply wish to share this revelation with you.

Simply stated, the answer to all of these questions about the meaning of human existence is *relationship in love*. The dictionary defines relationship as a connection or alliance by blood or marriage. A synonym of relationship is *kinship*. Both words denote intimacy and connection by birth or marriage with a common descent. Intimate spiritual relationship with God or another person can be called *fellowship*.

Hosea 4:6 says, "My people are destroyed for lack of knowledge." This is especially true in the area of relationships. You were created to be in relationship with other people. How can you experience victory in this life if you don't understand your very purpose for being? How can you build strong relationships if you do not know the principles involved? Is victory in this area eluding you? Lack of knowledge can destroy you; without it, what hope do you have?

If you agree that relationship is of the utmost importance and desire to build stronger relationships in your marriage as well as with God, family, and friends, then this study is meant just for you. In it you will find the good news of the gospel of Jesus Christ along with knowledge and understanding of God's blueprint for relationships that will minister to your heart.

As you read, keep your Bible close at hand. God's Word is essential to a proper understanding of the marital and relational principles revealed in this study. It alone contains all the pieces and the full solution to the puzzle of human existence and relationships. In order to derive the fullest possible benefit from this study, you must make it a high priority in your life. Don't rush through; take time to think about what you are learning. This study will: challenge you to find your true identity, potential and destiny; provide "homework" for further emotional and spiritual growth; offer practical "how-to" tips on applying the principles in your daily walk; suggest prayers and meditation to use for healing your heart in areas of your life in which the Holy Spirit brings conviction. You are embarking on an adventure that we hope you will thoroughly enjoy—a journey to discover your ultimate reality.

This study is designed as a basic foundational teaching tool for believers and non-believers alike, as well as for all leaders, especially at the church entry-level and in home-based cell groups. In whatever manner or setting you use for this study, our prayer for you is that the Holy Spirit will use the principles and scripture passages contained in this book to reveal to you personally truth that will change your life and help you build an *unshakeable marriage*. Finally, may your relationship with the Father, Son, and Holy Spirit be sealed and settled in your heart by the power of God and the blood of our Lord Jesus Christ.

How Best to Use This Book

1. Before you start, ask the Holy Spirit to help you understand everything He reveals to you.

2. This book is intended not for mere head knowledge but to minister to your inner spirit. Ask for the Holy Spirit's anointing to be upon the eyes and ears of your heart as you read.

3. This study is designed as progressive teaching, which means that learning proceeds one step at a time, building principle by principle. Don't proceed to the next chapter until you have learned the principles of the current chapter and begun applying them in your daily life.

4. Take your time. This study is not "fast food" but a gourmet meal designed to be eaten one bite at a time,

savored and allowed to digest; a feast to be enjoyed and meditated upon. It is seed in time-release capsule form that eventually, if allowed, will grow to maturity in your life. The various "courses" of this meal can be "eaten" more than once, and will reveal more truth each time you partake.

5. As you hear and understand truth from God's Word, be careful to obey by taking daily action to walk in its principles. It is not the hearers of the Word who are blessed, but the doers. The more you walk in God's ways, the more He will reveal Himself to you.

6. Only you can determine the benefits you will derive from this study. How much you learn will depend on how much you are willing to invest. The degree of your commitment to learn and change will determine the degree of benefit you receive.

7. Never close this book without praying that the things God has revealed to you to be healed in your heart.

8. This study will be of little value to you unless you are committed to the principles of repentance and forgiveness. The goal is spiritual growth, and repentance and forgiveness are prerequisites. As the Lord reveals areas of your life that are out of order, repent immediately and ask His forgiveness. Otherwise, positive change and growth will be impossible.

9. When discussing these principles with others and a need is revealed in their lives, don't let them leave without ministry or prayer. The ministry of the Holy Spirit is vital in this process of growth and change.

10. Remember always that Jesus is your focus. The truths and principles in this book are intended to point you to Him. Always ask Jesus how He would handle your situation and remember to thank Him for His everlasting love.

11. At the end of each chapter are two sections called *Principles of Covenant Life* and a *Prayer*. These principles are designed to help you become doers of the Word and not just hearers. These are foundational building blocks for practical application and effective living. Place them in your heart one at a time. Delete your wrong beliefs and replace them with God's ways and thoughts. The prayer is designed to minister to your heart and begin the healing process. Say the prayer in His presence.

Introduction

❧⨳❧

I'd like to take you back in time to the 1980s, to some of the events of my second marriage. First, however, I should share a little background information. I was born in 1946 and raised in the 50s. Being a "baby boomer" in the great environmental backdrop of Denver, Colorado was idyllic. Back then, Denver was a simpler city with clean air, little traffic and plenty of recreational areas for kids. We knew all the kids and families on our block at 50th & Grove Street. Our neighborhood could have been a set-piece for "Leave It to Beaver." Many of our friends looked and acted like they could have been cousins of Opie Taylor on "The Andy Griffith Show." Grade school was within walking distance and the beautiful summers seemed to last forever.

My high school actually was much like the movies "Grease" and "American Graffiti" combined. Sports, letter sweaters, girlfriends, going steady, pizza, dances, unparalleled music, and "fun, fun, fun" were the ingredients of our teenage days. At that time the sequence of life was birth, childhood, elementary school, high school, college (for some), marriage (for the majority), career, children, old age, death, and heaven (hopefully!) Then the cycle was complete. Most of us simply went from one to the next, much like a robot, never thinking outside that box.

Then, on one November day in 1963, as we sat in class, our whole world was shaken by a shattering announcement that came over the school's P.A. system: "President Kennedy has been assassinated." First came shock and then tears as grief and horror overcame everyone and penetrated to the very depth of our being. Within a year the deadly maelstrom of the war in Vietnam had reached America's shores. Our happy bubble of life in "Disneyland" had burst. The music had changed, and now the atmosphere of life was contaminated with fear and confusion. College students and recent high school graduates were drafted into the military by the thousands, dragged out of their comfortable desks and homes into either the jungles and rice paddies of Southeast Asia or the domestic battle zones of rebellious life in the "hood."

What had happened? An environmental "atomic bomb" had exploded, leaving an aftermath of destruction and devastation that could not be totally measured. It affected the heart, the philosophy, the spirituality, the morality and the integrity of our entire nation from the White House and the halls of Congress in Washington, through the statehouses and down every street of every community in America. In one way or another, war touched us all, affecting everyone and everything: our society, the church, our marriages, our families, and our children. War! Humanity's definitive failure! Even when it's over it's not over.

At some point within this same timeframe began the breakdown of the nuclear family and the abandonment of traditional family and moral values, aided by the influence of Hollywood, TV, and the erratic, dysfunctional lifestyles of many celebrities who had become bigger than life in our minds and who we had elevated to the status of heroes and role models. One byproduct of this was the culture of "no-fault" divorce which gave all of us an easy and supposedly painless way out of an uncomfortable marriage relationship.

Such massive changes in our society could not help but enter into the hearts of most Americans and influence their overall belief system. I was certainly no exception; I fell right into the snare of the divorce culture. Even though my training and schooling said otherwise, I bought enough of the lie to take me far down the highway of self-destruction. I got married for the first time at the end of my junior year in college. A year later, immediately after graduating, I was drafted into the U.S. Army and served in Vietnam for 14 months. My first daughter was only 6 months old when I left for Vietnam and my second daughter was born while I was there. I did not see her for the first time until I returned from Vietnam, when she was already 8 months old.

Even before the war I had become a confused and unstable young man. Now I was a Vietnam veteran trying to pick up with a marriage to a woman I felt I hardly knew and which now included two children I had never bonded with. Add to that the stress of my post-war emotional trauma and you have the makings of a tragedy. For the entire first year after 'Nam I was searching for answers to stop the questions calling out from my heart. I needed a healing when I didn't even know what a healing was. I began to look for something or someone to help me make sense of my new life that had become so complicated and so incompatible with the one I had left behind.

During this search my first marriage ended in divorce. I simply didn't have the personal character, the intestinal fortitude or even the knowledge of anything I could hold onto to keep me from sliding deeper into life's quicksand and eventually perishing.

Then, after many attempts and failures, I met the person who was to become my second wife. Little did I know at the time that the weight I carried in my heart from my past marriage and life experiences would one day impact my second marriage in such a negative way that another divorce would emerge. Without the healing of the still unanswered heart questions, patterns of thinking, and emotional cycles of the past, marital failure was inevitable. I was living one definition of insanity, believing that one day everything would be okay without my changing my heart or any of the other factors that had caused all my problems.

My past history and my wife's past history now collided. And what a collision it was! Ignorance added to ignorance equals...well, a bitter harvest. I hoped that she was the answer that would make sense of my existence and she hoped that I was the answer and security to her failure in past marriages and her help to heal her heart problems. What a mess it all was! I had two children from my first marriage who didn't live with me and my second wife had two children from a former marriage who did live with us. Yours, mine and ours! Talk about confusing! But our confusion was nothing compared to the confusion of the children. That was another time bomb ready to explode at any moment.

Often we would make love with each other and then turn around the same day and fight like bitter enemies. Human beings are supposed to be intelligent, but hurting the one you love is like feeding the dog while beating him with the newspaper. To say we were dysfunctional is a gross understatement.

Even my marriage vows contained an escape clause due to my faulty belief system regarding the marriage relationship. At the steps of a restaurant in front of a crowd of witnesses and in a ceremony performed by an ex-Catholic priest, I vowed to my bride: "As God is my witness, I promise to love Jill as long as I possibly can!" How short-sighted that oath was! But I could not see it at the time. That's how far off we were in our understanding. I had pledged to love Jill for as long as I possibly could. It was the best I could do. Unfortunately, my best wasn't good enough.

After ten years of a love-hate, wonderful-terrible, joyful-miserable roller-coaster ride marriage, I reached the end of "possibly." Today that vow sounds so ridiculous and immature, and it brought serious consequences. The whole situation was so late 70s, almost like a scene in a cheap B-movie, but the results were anything but funny. My second marriage ended in divorce.

Divorced again! What do I do now? I quickly plunged back into the world of chaos and confusion; back into the world of loneliness and darkness; back into the bars, the nightclubs and the beer. Was there nothing more to life than this? Who among us has never asked that question? The law of diminishing returns had been activated. What I was looking for could not be found in the bars or supplied by a woman. I felt like I was dying anew every day. Was there any hope for me? What about our kids, the innocent victims? What about my wife? I didn't have time to consider their plights. I was too wrapped up in my own self-pity. Where would I go from here?

Two years after the divorce I got a phone call from Jill, my second ex-wife. She sounded pretty good on the phone and, strangely enough, rather stronger than in the past. That fact caught my interest to the point where I continued listening to her even as she began to give me advice. She said, "Robert, what you need to do is to take two weeks off from going to the bars and carousing with your friends. Instead, try reading through the Gospel of John in its entirety. It is the Gospel of love. When you are finished reading it, give me a call."

Reluctantly, and with a few days of rebellious delay, I began reading John's Gospel just as Jill had suggested. When I finally reached the last verse of the last chapter, something happened to me in the emotional realm that I couldn't explain. I could only describe it as a peace, a sense of tranquility, an overall sense of ease that made me feel really good

That very same day I called Jill and we again began to reopen our lines of communication. One thing led to another and very soon we were living together—again. She moved in with me. We fought. She moved out. Later, I moved in with her. We fought some more and she was ready to throw me out. She even told me to pack my bags. Before I could leave, however, a friend of ours named Rita called me and said, "Robert, Jill is a mess. Would you consider coming to a marriage seminar at my church? She really needs you to be there." I told her yes. What I didn't know was that Rita had called Jill earlier and said, "Jill, Robert is a mess. Would you consider coming to a marriage seminar at my church? He really needs your help." Jill had also said yes. Both of us had agreed to come without knowing about the other.

We had been set up! By a Christian, no less! You know how aggravating *they* can be!

Well, we showed up on Friday night. The seminar had begun the day before, but Thursday was my day to play basketball and, as usual, my priority of self had overruled my obligation to be on time. As a result we didn't get to be in a group at the seminar because the groups had formed the first night. So, in the end it was just me, Jill and Rita all by ourselves, or so I thought.

That night Pastor Craig read Ephesians 6:12: "For we do not wrestle against flesh and blood, but against principalities, against powers, against the rulers of the darkness of this age, against spiritual hosts of wickedness in the heavenly places." The truth of that verse was exactly what I needed to hear to unlock and free me from what I had been dealing with in my heart since 1963.

What happened next was even more overwhelming.

Rita tried to get Jill and me to hold hands and pray. I didn't want to hold Jill's hand, especially since my bags were packed and I was on the verge of being thrown out of her house. She too refused to hold my hand, mainly due to the fact that we were arguing out loud right there in the middle of the church. We were seemingly oblivious to all the other people around us in their appointed groups who had now turned their heads and craned their necks and were listening to us in an almost frozen posture like the people in the E.F. Hutton commercials.

For her part, Rita was frantically praying and even started crying out loud, which only heightened the whole matter. (Later I found out that this kind of crying is called "travail.") Rita's prayer and the overall spiritual presence of the seminar fell on me and I began to repent to Jill for hurting her heart. Words that I didn't even know I had in me flowed effortlessly out of me from a source of which I had no knowledge. Those words were the exact words Jill needed to hear from me that unlocked the hurt that had built up in her over the years. They were things that only God and Jill knew were inside. We both started crying and then hugging. This was the beginning of our true reconciliation. (The power and source, we found out later, was the presence and the anointing of the Holy Spirit.)

Jill and I went back home and later that same night I saw a vision of someone carrying bags and suitcases and leaving our home through the front door. Upon a closer look, I realized that the departing figure was not me but the devil, stooped over dejectedly with his tail between his legs. Good riddance!

Not long after this, Jill and I decided to become members of that church. Through mentoring, training, and further ministry to our hearts, Pastor Craig introduced us into true

Introduction

Christianity and taught us God's principles of marriage relationship, which is called *covenant*. With this revelation of God's covenant, Jill and I renewed our wedding vows in 1990 with an awesome, Spirit-filled blood covenant ceremony. Since then, the Lord has completely restored our lives, our hearts, our family and our marriage.

Much like Saul, the bounty hunter of Christians, who through an encounter with the living Christ became Paul, the Christian life-giving apostle, Jill and I, failures in marriage and as parents became, by the anointing of the Holy Spirit, marriage rebuilders and ministers to the heart. All of this is to the glory of the Father, Jesus and the Holy Spirit to whom we have dedicated our marriage.

If you can relate to any part of our story; if you think there is no hope for you or for your children, then this book is for you. Jesus offers both the hope of the restoration of your marriage, your children, and your family as well as a brand new heart programmed with a new beginning. If you are preparing to enter marriage for the first time and want to get it right from the get-go, read this book. If you are interested in renewing your marriage vows, learning God's original plan, purpose, and blueprint for your relationship with Him and each other, and receiving all the blessings and promises that God has for you, read this book. Anyone—single, married, or divorced—who is interested in learning how to build strong biblical relationships should read this book. We make no guarantees; what happens in your relationships after reading this book is up to you and the people you are involved with. Some relationships may never be mended but, if all parties are in agreement, in Christ all things are possible!

I have already shared with you some of what marriage without covenant is like. In the pages that follow I will share with you our revelation of covenant and what biblical covenant relationship is like. At the close, I will share with you what our life has been like after covenant. It's an incredible and exciting ride, so get ready! Enjoy yourself! It's time!

Chapter 1

The Edenic Covenant: God's Original Plan

Following my second divorce I spent two years in darkness, confusion and ill health, literally living without a purpose. During that same period, however, I had a lot of time to think.

Proverbs 23:7 says, "For as [a man] thinks in his heart, so is he." Man, that's a scary thought! Did that mean I had become the sum total of my thoughts? Such dark thoughts filled my heart at that time. I thank God that no one could see on the outside a true picture of what my heart was like on the inside. If my outward appearance had reflected the way my heart felt inside, I would have looked like the portrait of "Dorian Gray!" Never mind what others thought; could I bear seeing myself in that condition?

1

Looking back on that period I can see now that I was a man without a foundation; a person of little character with nothing to stand on as I steadily lost my grip on sanity. Simply stated, I had a heart problem. I no longer knew who I was. I lacked direction, had no sense of where I was going and was full of where I had been. I was a mess! I could see but at the same time felt blind. With my job failing because of my poor attitude, I felt no mission or purpose in life. I had no plan, no vision and was losing my self confidence. Sound bleak? It was!

Where could I find the solution to my heart's cry? I felt so lonely then, but I know now that I was asking the same five universal heart questions that every human being on this planet seeks to answer:

1. "What is my true identity?" or "Who am I?"

2. "Who or what is my original source of being?" or "Where did I come from?"

3. "What is my destiny?" or "Where am I going?"

4. "What is my purpose?" or "What is the original intent for my very existence?"

5. "What is my potential?" or "What do I have the ability to do?"

Believe me, if you are facing these questions in your life, you will remain adrift in a sea of confusion until you find the answers. Some people never do. But don't despair; the answers are there. Help is available when you look in the right place.

The Journey Begins

To begin our revelatory journey searching for these heart answers, let's raise the curtain to Genesis chapter 1, where it all began, and look specifically for the hidden treasure found there:

> *Then God **said**, "Let **Us** make man in **Our image**, according to **Our likeness**; let them have **dominion** over the fish of the sea, over the birds of the air, and over the cattle, over **all** the **earth** and over every creeping thing that creeps on the earth"* (Genesis 1:26, emphasis added).

First of all, God the Father "said" or *spoke* His Word and by the power of that Word man was created. God is Spirit; therefore, His Word is also Spirit. The word "Us" refers to the divine Trinity of the Father, Son, and Holy Spirit, as does the possessive adjective "Our." There is one true God in three divine Persons, the ultimate Spirit relationship. They were all in agreement in this decision to make man. Here then is the answer to the question of our true origin and beginning. The Bible is crystal clear about where we came from: we were created by the spoken Word of God. He is our original *source.*

God created us in His own "image" and "likeness," and because He is Spirit we also are a spirit creation. "According to Our likeness" means we were created to function spiritually like God, living by faith in the power of His Word. Created in His likeness, we have been given some of the functions of His personality, namely a mind, a will and emotions, which we call a soul. With this definition we have

3

been given the biggest piece to the puzzle of our *identity*. Who are we? "A spirit man with a soul!"

Think about it! What an awesome reality it is to be created in the image and likeness of God Himself! When this truth finally hit me deep down in my heart, I saw the new me, with new priorities and a new sense of dignity and worth. What about you?

To have "dominion" over "all the earth" means to have authority to rule over this planet. God created us to rule over the created order. This provides us with another big piece to the puzzle because it touches on our *purpose* as well as our *potential*. Along with our authority to rule comes the power to carry out this responsibility to its completion. Do you think you are worthless with little of value to offer God or anyone else? Think again! God created you for dominion and authority. Knowledge of that truth should give you a greater perspective of your competence and responsibility.

> *And the Lord God formed man of the **dust** of the ground, and **breathed** into his nostrils the **breath of life**; and man became a **living being*** (Genesis 2:7, emphasis added).

God formed man's body from "dust" and by the power of the "breath" of the Holy Spirit man became a "living being." This "breath of life" started the flow of blood to all the systems and organs of man's body and he came to life. The Bible says that the life is in the blood (Lev. 17:11). It's a simple but profound truth: no blood, no life.

Totally assembled we are a *spirit* with a *soul* contained in a dirt *body*. We are therefore a three-part being similar to

4

the Trinity. The biggest difference, of course, is that we are the creation, not the Creator! Ultimately, God is our parent. In the beginning we, His children, were in relationship and connected by blood at birth and are His descendants! A family unit has been established! Any of us who are alive on the earth today have already won the "lottery" of life. We all have a chance at eternity, and God, our Father wants us with Him. From the

Totally assembled we are a spirit with a soul contained in a dirt body. We are therefore a three-part being similar to the Trinity.

very beginning, God established with man a covenant relationship by creation. Let's see what it looked like.

Eden

> *The Lord God planted a garden eastward in **Eden**, and there He put the man whom He had formed* (Genesis 2:8, emphasis added).

God first made a garden in a place called *Eden*, which means a *spot, place* or *presence*. Eden was the designated spot where man was to live in the continual presence of God. You might say it was a place where heaven touched earth. This *scene* (Eden) is where the *unseen* (God) communicated with the *seen* (man).

This garden of Eden contained "every tree...that is pleasant to the sight and good for food. The *tree of life* was also in the midst of the garden, and the *tree of the knowledge of good and evil*" (Gen. 2:9). Eden was the place designed for God's kingdom to be on earth as it was in heaven.

Here Comes the Command

God placed the man in the garden of Eden to "tend and keep it" (Gen. 2:15). This meant the man was given a "job" to cultivate the land and be a good steward not only over it but over all the animals as well. The next thing God said to the man—and why He said it—are of vital importance.

> *And the Lord God commanded the man, saying, "Of every tree of the garden you may freely eat; but of the* **tree of the knowledge of good and evil** *you shall not eat, for in the day that you eat of it you shall surely die"* (Genesis 2:16-17, emphasis added).

Why did God issue this command? This is one of the Scriptures that cause many people to conclude that God is a "tough hombre." Most children think their parents are mean for telling them no. In reality, appropriate discipline for training the heart of a child is a sign of a loving parent. In Eden God gave His child the opportunity to exercise his free will in choosing whether or not to obey that command. The man's choice would reveal whether or not he was acting in the true likeness of his Father. This decision to obey or not to obey, along with its accompanying consequences, was a maturing exercise in free choice given by a loving God who does not control or manipulate.

The two special trees in the garden represented the choice of life or death. Why these restrictions? This is how the "product" called man best functions. Maximum life function and relationship for man were subject to his obedience to the word of the King, his Father. Almost 6000 years later, the same trees of choice are available to each man: obey God and choose life, or disobey God and choose death.

In my own situation, this is where I first was experiencing darkness and death. I wasn't doing anything according to what my Father in heaven said. By default I was singing Frank Sinatra's song, "My Way." Since I had no idea of how to manage myself, I had no business trying to further manage a family or a mar-

Today, the same trees of choice are available to each man: obey God and choose life, or disobey God and choose death.

riage. At that time I had no clue how to relate properly to a woman. I needed to learn God's plan.

Now Enters the Woman

*And the Lord God said, "It is not good that man should be **alone**; I will make him a **helper comparable** to him"* (Genesis 2:18, emphasis added).

The man was "alone," a word that means "all-in-one" and/or "by himself". His "helper" would be comparable or equal to him. Genesis 1:27 says, that God created man "male and female." From this verse we understand that mankind was not created to be "all-in-one," but *two.*

And the Lord God caused a deep sleep to fall on Adam, and he slept; and He took one of his ribs, and closed up the flesh in its place. Then the rib which

7

the Lord God had taken from man He made into a woman, and He brought her to the man (Genesis 2:22-23).

From the one man God made one woman, or man with a "womb". She was already in Adam, as was the <u>seed</u> of all of mankind, and would carry this seed in her womb.

Notice that after Adam had been in relationship with God, had a job and a place to live, in that order, *God brought the woman to him.* Adam didn't have to go look for her! He didn't need a "little black book" or a palm pilot. He didn't have to cruise the internet. On the other hand, the woman didn't have to chase Adam every day in high school or look for him at the nightclubs. God presented the woman to him. All Adam had to do was sleep! The lesson here is that when we are in the proper relationship with God to hear His voice, He will take the responsibility to provide us with a good choice!

After seeing how God had initiated the relationship with him, Adam likewise initiated the first relationship with the woman. Just like his Father and in His presence, Adam said to his wife, "This is now bone of my bones and flesh of my flesh; she shall be called Woman, because she was taken out of Man" (Gen. 2:23). With these words Adam received the woman into his being as his equal. This was the first marriage vow ever recorded.

Continuing on to the next verse:

*Therefore a **man** shall **leave** his father and mother and be **joined** to his wife, and they shall become one flesh* (Gen. 2:24, emphasis added).

8

The principle here is that a man has to *leave* his parents for the purpose of being *joined* to his wife so the two of them can become one. Men, it says here that we are supposed to leave Mom and not create another mom but cleave to our wives. Ladies, it says that you need to leave Mom, too. That also means the telephone! *Ouch!* Instead of picking up the phone and calling "home" all the time, start depending on Jesus and share some of that communication with your husband. If nothing else, it will at least save on the long distance telephone bills!

If you are having problems cleaving, it usually involves not leaving.

If you are having problems *cleaving*, it usually involves not *leaving*.

Here's the Blessing

At this first wedding ceremony, God Himself instituted the custom of blessing the happy couple.

> Then God **blessed** them, and God said to them, "Be **fruitful** and **multiply**; fill the earth and **subdue** it; have **dominion**..." (Genesis 1:28, emphasis added).

When God blessed them with the parental blessing, it released them to leave to cleave. With that release they will be fruitful or prosperous in all they do, whether spiritually, physically, emotionally, or socially. The blessing of God also released them to multiply, not only in offspring, but also in everything they put their hand to. They have left one family unit to make another family unit. It is actually the parental blessing that initiates the proper leaving for cleaving.

This is the way marriage and family were designed originally to function. Once I learned this, I could see how doing things "My Way" had left God, His presence, and all of His blessings out of my marriage foundation. Predictably, my marriage produced no good fruit, no multiplication of prosperity, and exercised no dominion over anything.

We can see here in the first two chapters of Genesis the first two relationships:

1. God and man

2. Man and woman

God's way of relating to man is called *covenant.* He also designed marriage to be a covenant. This covenant God made with mankind in Eden is called, appropriately enough, the *Edenic Covenant.* What does this mean?

Covenant

The Bible is not a history book or a book of mythology but a book of covenants. It is divided into two sections, the Old Covenant and the New Covenant or the Old and New Testaments, as we know them today. The Old Testament contains seven major covenants, seven being a divine number meaning "completion." An eighth covenant is found in the New Testament. Eight is a divine number that means "new beginning."

Perhaps we can better define and understand a covenant by looking at its early components. The following check list indicates the elements comprising a covenant. Every component should be present for the covenant to be valid. With each point I have included an evaluation of how my definition of marriage stacked up prior to my divorce.

A covenant relationship contains the following prerequisites (every one is essential):

1. It must take place in the presence of God and thus is considered sacred and holy unto the Lord. *(I blew that one!)*

2. It must take place between at least two parties. (Marriage requires three—a man, a woman, and God). *(Oops! I missed that one too. I left out God.)*

3. The parties must be in agreement. *(Wrong again! We argued over so many things. The only thing we always agreed on is that we both loved me!)*

4. The party who decides to make the covenant is called the covenant initiator and will speak first. The covenant initiator usually is the stronger of the two parties and becomes the more responsible. *(Nope. I spoke first, but being the more responsible party mostly eluded me.)*

5. The person receiving the covenant is called a covenant partner. *(Okay, my wife passed this one, but was only as good as my poor leadership.)*

6. The covenant initiator's word becomes his bond or vow. *(Failed. My "vow" to love her "as long as I possibly could" had a built-in escape clause. See Introduction.)*

7. The covenant initiator's word always contains a promise or promises. *(I blew this one, too. I did not keep my word or my promise to love and not leave her.)*

8. This word is unbreakable and also irrevocable. *(Failed; that's a "no-brainer!")*

9. An exchange of something of value always takes place. *(Missed by a mile. I never exchanged love or my heart because I did not know love until I asked Jesus into my heart to be Lord. I didn't have love until I had Jesus.)*

10. The attitude of the parties was that their very lives were at stake and they would rather die than break this agreement. *(Are you kidding? My attitude was, "If the pain overcomes the pleasure, I'm outta here!")*

11. The attitude from one's very heart is, "All I am and all I have are yours." *(Maybe so, but that wasn't a very good deal for her at the time.)*

12. Usually the establishment of a covenant was followed by a celebration of some kind, such as a meal. *(Finally, I passed one! I never missed a meal!)*

As you can see, on that test I went down in flames! My marriage failed and everyone got hurt from the children to the grandparents. Today it is easy to see why from the very beginning my marriage was headed for total collapse. My marriage failed because it had a leadership problem—me.

How many of these components of a covenant relationship are still missing in your marriage? Today it's easier to get a marriage license than a driver's license. If driver training comes with a manual, why doesn't marriage? *It does.* The Bible is our marriage manual, written by the expert—God—who invented marriage in the first place. Who better to instruct us in the ways of marriage than the original designer? Pick up the Bible. It's never too late to return to God's original blueprint and incorporate those missing components.

As stated in the preface, we are all searching for our true identity. However, before we come to know who we are, we need to know more of who God is. **As we see** and understand more of God's ways, His thoughts, His personality, His nature, His principles, His character and His Word, we will get closer to Him. The closer we come to understanding His identity, the more He will define *ours*. His identity can be defined in one word—*love*.

The Bible is our marriage manual, written by the expert—God—who invented marriage in the first place.

Where is Love?

Beloved, let us love one another, for love is of God; and everyone who loves is born of God and knows God. He who does not love does not know God, for **God is love** (1 John 4:7-8, emphasis added).

God is Love! Just think of the implications! Since this is true about the Creator, then everything He created, and especially our relationship, came from Love, the Author. Everything in Eden was a love portrait from the greatest Artist of all—the Ancient of Days! It was not in His nature to create anything contrary to love. Perfect love has only love. Did Adam and Eve know perfect love? Not yet. Did they have any questions about their identity thus far? Not yet. Up to this point there was no flaw in them. There was no sin! They were in covenant marriage relationship training, eventually to be rooted and grounded in love! They were a work in progress. While in process they were being blessed. Blessing is love manifested. God lovingly blessed them with:

- the gift of Life

- the beginnings of a relationship with Him

- the beginnings of a relationship with each other

- the provision of food, water, real estate in the suburbs with a great view, precious minerals, pets, etc.

- a job

- dominion over the earth

- glorious, healthy bodies

- superior minds, will, and emotions

- a dynamic spirit

- healthy hearts

- (the list could go on and on, but you catch my drift!)

With all those blessings, don't tell me that God is not love or that one commandment was too tough to keep!

Eden was a happening spot! Everybody on earth showed up there. Man functioned at his best there in the presence of God! He was a free moral agent given all the authority on earth to rule as a king. He literally had everything he could possibly need. He could do everything he needed to do. He was equipped spiritually and physically with every function necessary to accomplish his purpose. He could be a gourmet if he so chose or go for fast food. He could travel about the earth as he willed. He was naked and was not ashamed! This meant he never had to go shopping for clothes with his wife! She could arrange her house anyway she liked without an argument. He was learning to be the ultimate romanticist with her! What a deal! They could do everything, go anywhere, have everything, eat anything, touch anything, see everything...with the exception of one little tree!

Principles of Covenant Life

(to be discussed in home groups for practical application)

1. Our identity comes in direct proportion to the extent of our commitment to and knowledge of our relationship with God and His Word. Isaiah 55:8-9.

2. Our purpose is to have dominion and establish God's kingdom on earth as it is in heaven. Herein also lies our potential. God will equip you with all the ability needed to carry out your purpose. Gen. 1:26.

3. God's Word will accomplish that which it was sent out to do. It will not return to Him void. Isaiah 55:11.

4. God's purpose for us is His will. His will is found in His Word. His Word is His will. God's Character and His Word are one! What He has said is unbreakable and irrevocable.

5. All God is and all He has is available to us.

6. God is the only one, true, original God, and we too must be our one, true, and original selves and not try to be anyone else.

7. We can only function at our maximum in the presence of God. That is, our spirit must be connected to its source, His Spirit. John 15:5.

15

8. Spiritually, male and female were created equal! Identity, destiny, potential, and purpose of each are the same.

9. A family unit is God's design and blueprint. For maximum efficiency, a man must leave his parents to cleave to his wife. Leave to cleave!

10. Everything God created by the power of the authority of His Word has order in it for maximum life and efficiency.

Questions for Further Thought

1. To what extent do *you* draw your identity from your relationship with God and His Word?_____ _____What can you do to grow in this area?_____

   _____

2. Have you truly left your parents to cleave to your spouse? _____ If not, what's holding you back?_____

   _____

Prayer

(Repeat this prayer out loud and/or add your own when led)

Holy Spirit, come, help me to pray!

Father, Almighty God, Creator of all things seen and unseen! I thank You for the revelation in Your Word. I thank You for loving me and giving my precious life to me. Father, I want to know You more! I want to be in intimate fellowship with You!

To You alone, God, I give permission to tell me "who I am." I have allowed parents, friends, and other people to give me my identity. I see now that this is wrong. I forgive all of those who I have allowed to define me _____(names)_____ Thank You for Your forgiveness. From this day forward help me to hear only what You say about me.

Plant deep in my heart, God, Your Word and the Truth of my real identity, my real destiny, and my real purpose for being.

Lord, I thank You for giving me dominion over all things! I choose to exercise that authority today. Help me be a good steward of all that You have entrusted to my care to tend and cultivate, especially Your children.

Help me to be obedient to every Word that proceeds out of Your mouth. Teach me humility to respond in choice always to Jesus, the tree of life.

Thank You, Lord for all of my blessings! Amen!

Chapter 2

The Adamic Covenant: God's Restoration Plan Announced

⁂

J ust that one little tree! The only thing that man was told *not* to do! Why are we always fascinated by the things we know *not* to do? Do *not* smoke. Do *not* try marijuana. Do *not* use cocaine. Do *not* have sex before marriage. Do you suppose that the negative word "not," used in a command, is a warning of negative consequences? Is it possible that "not" could be given in love and wisdom to help prevent any adverse result? If so, why do we continually overlook that word "not" and proceed to make the wrong choice?

Let's be honest; I've done it so many times and suffered the consequences that I'm embarrassed to admit it. And you have too. It's an affliction common to man. Every day all over the world it happens, from the ghetto to the mansion and from the statehouse to the White House. It happens to men and women both great and small, and also to children. It happens to even the greatest of leaders. The results are always the same. You might say it's the law of "spiritual gravity": whatever rises too high must come down. Proverbs 16:18-19 says: "Pride goes before destruction, and a haughty spirit before a fall. Better to be of a humble spirit with the lowly, than to divide the spoil with the proud."

If it happens to everybody, let's see how it began with the first human couple.

Adam, the first man and the first leader, was in a position of dominion. His job was going pretty well and his relational training was almost complete, to the point where he might have started taking his blessings for granted. Can you relate to that? I can. Just about the time you think you have it made, all of a sudden the floor drops out from under you and you crash and burn! All because you left Jesus out of the picture. Anyone who has ever been demoted, fired, divorced, jilted, thrown into jail or experienced any number of other setbacks remembers only too well the heat and pain of the torment! This is what happened to Adam one day. His violation of one little "not" affected the future of all mankind and brought down a universal death sentence!

The First Temptation

It all began, simply enough, with a conversation:

*Now the serpent was more cunning than any beast of the field which the Lord God had made. And he said to the woman, "Has God indeed **said,** 'You shall **not** eat of every tree of the garden'?" And the woman said to the serpent, "We may eat of the fruit of the trees of the garden; but of the fruit of the **tree** which is in the midst of the garden, God has **said,** 'You shall **not** eat it, nor shall you touch it, lest you die.'" Then the serpent said to the woman, "**You will not surely die. For God knows that in the day you eat of it your eyes will be opened, and you will be like God, knowing good and evil**"* (Genesis 3:1-5, emphasis added).

Here enters the villain into this love story: Satan! He indwells the serpent and speaks through it. His plan is to tempt and to deceive the woman for the purpose of destroying the engagement and courting period of God and man, thereby stealing the pleasure and glory they would have otherwise shared in consummating this relationship.

Unfortunately, evil already existed as evidenced by the mention of the *tree* of the knowledge of good and evil. We know evil was birthed by an act of Satan. God did not create Satan; He created *Lucifer*, who was a most splendid cherub. Because of his overweening pride, Lucifer became Satan after he chose to commit high treason against God. Like all created beings, Lucifer was subject to the spiritual law of gravity. His pride lifted him too high, and so he fell. (See Isaiah 14:12-15; Ezekiel 28:11-19.)

Notice Satan's subtle strategy. He first checked to see if the woman *knew* what God had said. Every time the

Word of God comes to man, Satan will immediately give a counterfeit alternative and try to steal that Word. At the time, Satan's counterfeit always *seems* to be a better choice. Over the short term it seems worthy of consideration but is laced with evil and leads to death in the long term. Unlike God's Word, which has the power to deliver what it promises, Satan's counterfeit word contains promises he can't deliver—and has no intention of delivering. Satan is a fraud and his word is deceptive. He's good at marketing lies and making promises he will never fulfill. All of his "commercials" try to convince us that we want something or, better yet, need something. After we fall for it and spend more than we can afford to get it, we discover too late either that we already had it or didn't need it in the first place.

After Satan's challenge to God's Word, the woman faced two choices: "you will surely die" or "you will not surely die." Which one was the truth and which one was the lie? Her first option was to trust the Word and character of God her Creator. Her second option was to trust the word and character of Satan, the father of lies. The choice should have been a no-brainer: God and His Word had a perfect track record with them while Satan had absolutely no credentials to recommend him.

The tempter said, "...in the day you eat of it your eyes will be opened." What a laugh! Satan offered her sight when she could already see! Then Satan promised her that she would become "like God." She already *was* like God, having been created in His image and likeness. Satan promised her that she would know good and evil. What advantage is there to knowing evil? Can you see how empty Satan's words were? He could never deliver on what he said; all he could do was tempt, and he was an expert in that department.

Don't be too hard on Eve; we all fall for those same old lines all the time. Why? Don't tell me it's all Satan's fault. We have free choice.

The very next verse gives us a clue why Eve fell so easily (and why we do too):

> So when the woman saw that the tree was **good for food**, that it was **pleasant to the eyes**, and a tree **desirable to make one wise**, she took of its fruit and ate. She also gave to her husband with her, and he ate (Genesis 3:6).

Whenever we try to function outside the authority and life of God's Word, we enter into the kingdom of the prince of darkness, Satan, where only flesh and death abide. Flesh is the condition of putting s-e-l-f before God. That turns everything around: s-e-l-f becomes f-l-e-s before-h, Jehovah God. This relationship never works! We become our own god and the true God of the universe is dethroned in our heart. The Bible calls this counterfeit kingdom the "world," a place where nothing is as it seems:

> For all that is in the world—the lust of the flesh, the lust of the eyes, and the pride of life—is not of the Father but is of the world (1 John 2:16).

In our counterfeit kingdom we have traded love, which never fails and always satisfies, for lust, which always fails and never satisfies. Lust serves only self, usually at the expense of others. It is an overmastering desire that is opposed to our God-given spirit within. Lust always turns us around and away from God. Eve saw that the tree was good for food—to satisfy self, the lust of the flesh; pleasant to the eyes—to gratify self, the lust of the eyes; and desirable to make one wise—to justify self, the pride of life.

Where was Adam?

This is the part I dislike the most. Adam was *with* her and he ate! He simply sat on his *self* and passively watched the entire scene! If only he had been aggressive in the face of Satan, exercised his authority and dominion over the snake and told his wife, *"Not!"* After all, that's what a responsible covenant initiator is required to do! Just like Adam, this is what I failed to do when my marriage and family were at stake! I was passive and selfish when I should have stood and taken authority over evil while it was still only in my thought life. That same iniquity of Adam, however, is what every man has inherited to this day as a flaw in character! Passivity in the face of deception and temptation prevailed instead of boldness in exercising his authority over all things! And it gets worse from here!

In our counterfeit kingdom we have traded love, which never fails and always satisfies, for lust, which always fails and never satisfies.

Not only did man get turned around here, but also he got turned upside down and separated from God! Note this, however: *God did not withdraw His love, man separated*

24

himself from God through his own choice. Man was created a three-part being: spirit, soul, and body. The spirit was designed to be the master. The soul was the servant to the spirit, the master whom it obeyed, while the body did whatever the spirit and soul dictated. This order works! But after Adam and Eve ate the fruit, Adam's selfish flesh became the master. His soul became servant to the flesh, the master whom it obeyed. The spirit was detached from its divine power source, the Holy Spirit, and became completely dysfunctional.

Man's three-part being now became subject to the Word of God: "...for in the day that you eat of it you shall surely die" (Gen. 2:17). Let's get it straight as to what to "die" really means. Since God is man's life source, apart from Him all our systems fail. As Genesis 3:7 shows, however, after Adam and Eve sinned their body and soul were still functioning: "Then the *eyes* of both of them were *opened*, and they *knew* that they were naked; and they *sewed* fig leaves together and made themselves coverings" (Gen. 3:7 emphasis added). Prior to their sin, they did not have to rely on their senses to see from without, but could see by the spirit from within! They were to be trained from the inside out, not from the outside in.

The moment they violated God's command they were immediately unplugged from their source of power! The absence of the spirit severely affects the soul (the mind, will and emotions) of this human being because it no longer has its original master! Eventually the body will cease its activity and go back to the ground from which it was taken. Our body can die and return to dust but our spirit and soul cannot totally be terminated. Remember, our spirit and soul were created in God's image and likeness by His Word and His Word will never pass away. Death, in spiritual terms, means to be apart from God. The spirit and soul suffered spiritual death. The body was sentenced to its natural death, which might take many years to come to pass.

Adam and Eve had sinned. What does that mean? Very simply, they responded contrary to what God's Word commanded. The wages of sin is death, both spiritual and natural (see Rom. 6:23).

The eating of that fruit represented biting into the package containing the entire belief system of the kingdom of darkness.

"Isn't that penalty a little harsh?" you might ask. Not really. Why? It was actually the natural consequence of their act of disobedience. The eating of that fruit represented *biting into the package containing the entire belief system of the kingdom of darkness.* Breaking God's command didn't cause the death; eating the poison in the package did. God's Word is life! It's who He Is! Life is the defining characteristic of His kingdom. The defining characteristic of the kingdom of darkness is death. When Adam and Eve chose to eat what God had forbidden they chose death over life. Their penalty might seem harsh at first, but it is, in the end, ultimate reality—the natural consequence of their choice.

Have you ever wondered: "What if Adam and Eve had apologized and repented to God after sinning? Would He have been merciful and perhaps given them a break?" Unfortunately, that's not what happened. Adam and Eve chose to play the "blame game."

*And they heard the sound of the Lord God walking in the garden in the cool of the day, and Adam and his wife **hid** themselves from the presence of the Lord God among the trees of the garden. Then the Lord God called to Adam and said to him, "**Where are you**?" So he said, "I heard your voice in the garden, and I was afraid because I was naked; and I hid myself"* (Genesis 3:8-10 emphasis added).

Hiding makes it evident that Adam and Eve clearly knew in their hearts that they had disobeyed and were not seeking God to offer any sort of explanation. I don't think God, who knows everything, was seeking Adam's location when He asked, "Where are you?" Could it be that God was asking the covenant initiator, "Where are you in this matter with regard to your responsibility?' Or was He asking, "Where are you in your heart with this decision?" Is it possible that with the fruit of evil inside Adam that a Holy God chose not to see sin? Whatever the case, God then asked, "Who told you that you were naked? Have you eaten from the tree which I commanded you that you should not eat?" (Gen. 3:11) God already knew the answer to that one too; He is God! Can you see the opportunity God gave man to be accountable for his sin and to show some act of contrition?

Instead, Adam replied to God's question with an accusation: "The woman whom you gave to be with me, she gave me of the tree and I ate" (Gen. 3:12). Rather than accepting accountability or expressing remorse, he blamed his wife! Men are no different today; we all play the blame game.

God likewise gave Eve an equal opportunity by asking her, "'What is this you have done?' And the woman said, 'The serpent deceived me and I ate'" (Gen. 3:13). This was another poor choice of words on her part that revealed her heart attitude. Like Adam she did not ask for forgiveness but tried to assign blame, this time to the snake! "The devil made me do it!" Sorry lady; that excuse didn't work then and it doesn't work today! The Bible says we are accountable for our choices. The devil cannot make us do anything. All he can do is tempt and deceive: "But each one is tempted when he is drawn away by his own desires and enticed. Then, when desire has conceived, it gives birth to sin; and sin, when it is full-grown, brings forth death" (James 1:13-15).

"O.K. I'm bored this afternoon. I think I'll do my own thing today, blindfold my heart and conscience, take off for a little excitement, go somewhere scintillating and maybe look at some new scenery or meet someone provocative that I'm not supposed to. I'll just leave a little early from work today. Besides, she's going to be late tonight anyway. I think I'll call the wife right now, tick her off a little, so if I have a few beers and come home late I'll tell her I needed to let off a little steam. You know, make her think it's her fault I'm not home and had to drink. You know the little games people play."

"Hey, this looks like a happening place. Here I am. Give me a Budweiser, please. Hey, you see that woman sitting over there by herself? Buy her a drink too. Tell her it's from me. Wonder what she's thinking? She's smiling big time at me for that drink. Guess I'll just go by on the way to the restroom and say hello. What's up? No, I'm not married, are you?

"What are you doing here tonight? Oh, really, me too. You're cute. Oh, you think so, thanks.

"She went to the restroom. I wonder what she's thinking about me? I'll bet you I could score tonight, if I wanted to. You know you're married bubba. Shut up, I don't want to think about that now. Here she is again. Well, I got to go, it's getting late. You say you would like me to stop by for a nightcap. Sure, where do you live? O.K. I'll follow you."

Can't you see, it wasn't the devil that made me do that. Sin is premeditated. It starts with one thought and if not stopped, it will run its full course. If sin is not stopped it will bring forth a degree of death to all the players. Are you still falling for that age-old temptation? And you consider yourself to be listed in the same category as a species called "homo sapiens?"

Any fool can play the pre-divorce game.

Covenant

God and His Word are one. His Word is His covenant. If we reject His Word, we reject Him! Rejection of God's Word brings death! Since Adam and Eve had rejected the Edenic Covenant, God responded with what is called the Adamic Covenant, the first in a series of covenants containing God's restoration plan for mankind to return to His original plan in Eden. God relates to man solely according to the parameters He sets within covenant. The Adamic covenant did not invalidate the Edenic Covenant, which will never pass away, but was God's response to the consequence of man not receiving the Edenic covenant.

Now Enter the Curses

Give special notice to the following curses that resulted. When we don't receive God's love, which contains life and blessing, by default we receive the counterfeit, which contains death and curses. Here is the Adamic covenant:

> *So the Lord God said to the serpent: "Because you have done this, you are **cursed** more than all cattle, and more than every beast of the field; on your belly you shall go, and you shall eat dust all the days of your life, and I will put **enmity between you** and the **woman**, and between your seed and her **Seed**; He shall **bruise** your **head**, and you shall **bruise** His **heel**"* (Genesis 3:14-15 emphasis added).

Enmity means that man and Satan will be enemies. The devil will enjoy limited power as he bruises only the heel of man. Man's *Seed*, however will bruise Satan's head. This "Seed" is a prophetic reference to the coming of the Messiah, or the Savior of man, whose name we know is Jesus, to destroy the works of the devil. Glory to God! Man was given this promise to live until his Seed restored dominion to man because God's will shall be done according to His Word to accomplish its original purpose! Man's dominion was stolen by Satan, who had authority to have dominion in his kingdom of darkness in which man now became a citizen.

The Adamic covenant continued:

To the woman He said: "I will greatly multiply your sorrow and your conception; In pain you shall bring forth children; Your desire shall be for your husband, and he shall rule over you"(Genesis 3:16).

The curses are as follows:

1. The entire human race will be conceived with having to face sorrow and death.

2. All women will have pain from the day they give birth to their children and that pain, as we know, will continue in the heart of woman throughout her life on earth.

3. Her desire shall be for her husband instead of her God, finding her needs not able to be met. When I see a woman who is physically, emotionally, or verbally abused time after time and yet goes back to the same abusive situation I want to ask, "Don't you realize you are laboring under that curse?" Some men take advantage of that desire of the woman to stay with them, and control and manipulate her human spirit.

4. She lost the rule and dominion she once shared equally with the man and became subject to him ruling over her! Now she goes to the man asking him to tell her how valuable she is, asking him for her identity, only to hear all the things she is lacking according to him. Terrible situation! This problem is all too prevalent today!

Now consider the man's curses. God said to Adam:

31

Cursed is the ground for your sake; In toil you shall eat of it all the days of your life. Both thorns and thistles it shall bring forth for you, and you shall eat the herb of the field. In the sweat of your face you shall eat bread till you return to the ground, for out of it you were taken; for dust you are, and to dust you shall return (Genesis 3:17-19).

Man is sentenced to hard labor for the rest of his life to sweat and toil to survive. After a life of cultivating the ground, he will physically die and decompose back to dust. Contrary to the popular perception of many regarding work, to have a job is a blessing. It's a privilege to work. Avoiding work is the curse. Thinking you're going to start at the top and never at the bottom is a lie. If you think work is a curse, you're under it.

The Consequences of Choosing the Wrong Tree—the Fruit of the Kingdom of Darkness

The following is only an abbreviated list of what was released through sin. Remember, eating of the fruit of that tree meant eating its deadly poison.

1. **A spirit of fear.** They were detached from perfect love. They were afraid and hid themselves because they were naked. They lost some kind of covering that they had enjoyed before. I believe it was the hand and glory of God that covered them before, that came with the covenant relationship for protection. Covenant initiators are bound by their word to protect their partner's life. They now were subject to all fears including a

daily fear of death and abandonment. What are your fears? Getting old? Dying? Lack? Being alone?

2. **A spirit of guilt.** Every day they had to live with the mistake they had mad. They lost confidence in their potential.

3. **A spirit of shame.** They felt they were a mistake and had to cover up their nakedness. Their true sense of identity had been turned upside down and inside out! "I'll never live up to or become what I would like to be. I'll always fall short."

4. **A spirit of rebellion.** They rebelled against the Word of God and therefore to His authority. Rebellion is simply saying yes when God says no.

5. **A spirit of pride.** The counterfeit trinity: *me, myself,* and *I*, also known as the "I" disease. Pride is two-faced: it manifests in either arrogance or self-pity. Both of these positions are diametrically opposed to God! Pride is self-centered, not God-centered.

6. **A spirit of rejection.** When you reject God's Word which contains life, you are left with death, which is the rejection of life. "No one loves me."

7. **A deaf and dumb spirit.** This spirit prevents us from hearing and listening or even believing the word of anyone in authority. We have the ability to hear but don't want to.

8. **A spirit of performance.** Man, who has lost his identity, will strive and be driven to prove his true worth by his own performance, or works, like by becoming "religious."

9. **A spirit of Lethargy.** Some will choose non-performance instead: lethargy, laziness, apathy or procrastination. "Who cares? I don't give a rip!"

10. **A spirit of bondage.** Man no longer is free because he has left his parents (God) improperly, in rebellion, and thereby forfeits the blessing of prosperity. This actually binds him to the parent (God). So, with improper *leaving* comes the inability for proper *cleaving* in the relationships that follow.

11. **A spirit of idolatry.** We can become the "I"-doll or we will substitute "other gods" to worship to fill the "void" left by the loss of the one true God.

12. **A spirit of lust.** Now man's kingdom runs itself by means of lust, the counterfeit of love. Everything and everybody are now considered only objects. These objects have lost their intrinsic value and worth and are labeled now by their external appearance only. Man's prevailing attitude is, "If it looks good, or it feels good, do it"! Sensuality has replaced spirituality.

Let's not go on! You get the picture.

What I didn't realize, and what most people do not realize, is that everyone who does not receive Jesus as Lord and Savior to destroy the works of this package are being influenced by this entire list by default. Why are more than 50% of marriage relationships on the road to divorce? The same reason mine was. For lack of knowledge we are being destroyed (see Hos. 4:6). Knowledge of what? Read on.

The Great Consequences of Choosing "The Tree of Life"—the Fruit of the Kingdom of Light

The most overlooked factor in the Edenic Covenant was the other tree in the garden, the tree of life. In case you don't fully recognize its significance, let me explain. We have seen that the tree of the knowledge of good and evil represented a choice. We have seen also that to choose that tree was to choose death. Obviously, the other tree represents what its name expresses: *life.*

> *Then the Lord God said, "Behold, the man has become like one of Us, to know good and evil. And now, lest he put out his hand and take also the tree of **life**, and **eat**, and **live forever**"*—*therefore the Lord God sent him out of the garden of Eden to till the ground from which he was taken* (Genesis 3:22-23 emphasis added).

My friends, this tree of life was **JESUS!** Jesus said of Himself, "He who *eats* this bread will *live forever*" (Jn. 6:58). As with every other human being without exception, Adam and Eve must also have knowledge and choose the person of Jesus Christ in response to a covenant relationship with God. Jesus was there in the beginning, as was the Holy Spirit, whose fruit it was on that tree. If you don't choose Jesus and the Holy Spirit, you haven't chosen the Father, either, who is One with them in the Trinity. Wherever One is, the whole family relationship is! They are three distinct persons and personalities but are inseparable as a family unit! Today we cannot know the Father without the ministry of Jesus, and cannot know Jesus without the ministry of the Holy Spirit. Today, get to know the Holy Spirit. He's here right now, with you, revealing this truth! Welcome Holy Spirit! We want to know You more!

For Restoration, Redemption and Covering, We Need the Blood

Finally, but of paramount importance, was God's loving provision for the sinning couple: "Also for Adam and his wife the Lord God made tunics of skin, and clothed them" (Gen. 3:21). God, being the more responsible covenant party, continued to offer them protection with a temporary covering of animal skin. What is important to see here is that He had to sacrifice the life of an animal to use its skin to cover them. The blood of that animal was shed and still fresh on the skin. Remember, the life was in the blood! The animal slain was most likely a lamb. You see, Jesus from whom all life came, is there always offering us life. Was not the blood of life in man in the first covenant in Eden?

The tree of life was JESUS!

The covenant offered in Eden could be called an attempt on the part of God to give His life to mankind by eating of the "tree of life" after already giving man life by the breath of the Holy Spirit so as to be related by blood. We are going to call the covenant in Eden a "blood" covenant. Even though Adam and Eve did not receive it because they left out Jesus, someone from their *seed* will make it again a reality. The Adamic covenant, with the temporary blood covering, will have to suffice until God's Word becomes manifest! This too was a blood covenant. The promise of the "Seed" carries with it the *hope* and *gospel* of the future.

36

He has delivered us from the power of darkness and translated us into the kingdom of the Son of His Love, in whom we have redemption through His Blood, the forgiveness of sins (Colossians 1:13-14).

Do not love the world or the things in the world. If anyone loves the world, the love of the Father is not in him. For all that is in the world—the lust of the flesh, the lust of the eyes, and the pride of life—is not of the Father but is of the world (1 John 2:15-16).

I am the door. If anyone enters by Me, he will be saved, and will go in and out and find pasture (John 10:9).

The Tree of Life, Jesus, is the only way back into the kingdom of God.

Communication

(topics for marriage or group discussions)

When man fell, the greatest consequence in this breach of relationship was the immediate loss of the direct line of communication he had shared with God. Removed from this spiritual connection to God and his source of life, man suffered alienation from and insensitivity to the voice and Word of God. Now he had to rely on the knowledge of his five senses, where before he had been learning to hear from within his subconscious spirit mind, his heart.

This loss of communication with God of course affected his marriage communication with his wife. That same loss still troubles marriages today. We have communication problems on a daily basis with each other and are like ships passing in the night unaware of each other's thoughts, feelings, or the meanings in their words. My second divorce was due to the breakdown of communication from heart to heart. Communication breakdown continues to be one of the primary causes of divorce today.

One obvious example of this, and one of the most common impasses in marital communication, is the attitude: "I'm right and you're wrong." It doesn't matter what the subject is. One person has to be right at the expense of the other person being wrong. While you are busy communicating the reasons you are right and your spouse is wrong, what is going on in the atmosphere of the heart? Why does one always feel hurt if the other proves to be right? Because that way of communicating comes from the tree of the knowledge of good and evil. So, what's so bad about that? The problem with that tree is that it can never bring life. It brings only death and victimization. You may be perfectly correct, but your correctness will never minister life or communicate life to the other person.

Let's talk! Here are some principles that should be considered for improving our communication skills and understanding ourselves and the opposite sex in relationship.

Man gets his adequacy from what he *does*. He understands things according to how it relates to his job, work, career, sports, hobbies, etc. He is a human "doing" instead of a human being. Are you "caught up" in what you are doing? Does this send a relational message to your spouse that she is a lower priority to you than your doings? Do you think she will open her heart to that scenario? Unlikely. How about stopping from time to time and talking to her about things other than what you are doing? If she feels like she is a low

38

priority to you, she will find something or someone who tells her otherwise.

Woman gets her adequacy from her *many relationships* or with whom she has heart relationships. She is a relational being. Ladies, are you consumed with what all the other girls think and say about you? Have you made your kids, grandkids, friends or extended family more important than your husband? If so, this is what you have been communicating to your husband's heart.

Man gets his adequacy from what he does; woman, from her many relationships.

Most men communicate on a *topical* level, that is, on the level of the conscious mind, from primarily his brain. He believes all issues can be dealt with on that logical mental level. Men, we need to understand that women like the details and sometimes they only want us to listen and not always try to fix things.

On the flip side, most women communicate from a *relational* level, that is, on the level of how everything affects her emotions or her heart. Ladies, be aware that your husband has been trained by tradition not to feel those things. You are his helpmate to teach him how to feel. That takes practice and patience and time.

In the complexities of this 21st Century, we must have knowledge and understanding to read between the lines in communication. We must realize there are always those two levels of communication going on at all times and learn to be sensitive to the differences between men and women as to how they perceive these levels. Neither person's perception is right or wrong, just different. Appreciate and acknowledge the differences. My suggestion for improving the flow of the conversation is to ask the Holy Spirit's help before communicating.

Only 20 % of all communication is verbal; the other 80% is non-verbal. What we say with body language and facial expressions is perceived on both the topical and relational levels. Ask yourself, how is this affecting the other's heart? We knew a couple where the woman would not forgive her husband's adulterous affair. Unforgiveness stopped all deep heart communication and manifested itself in her body language until the marriage eventually died. When communication dies, so does the relationship.

We need to be aware of an ongoing romantic level of communication daily in every marriage relationship. It's an invisible flowing river that brings life daily to that relationship. Words of blessing and loving actions feed the affection needed by the woman and stimulate the sexual expression needed by the man and are directly associated with all the above principles. Without knowledge of this, the fire of romance goes out. Good communication is both an art and sexual foreplay. See the need. Get a plan. Communicate.

I have found that the sexual level of communication only flows in direct proportion to the knowledge of all the things we have talked about. To meet each others physical, emotional and spiritual needs, we must learn good communication skills and put them into practical application. To begin with, back up if you have to and redefine your most common relational terms and explain what you mean by them. Be able to give God's biblical definition for things of importance where the heart is concerned. That will give you a solid foundational basis for agreement and growth in compatibility.

Without knowledge today we can dishonor our spouse by how we communicate. Our words have power to honor, bless and be a source of life to the other. Be a good listener, that's why you have two ears and only one mouth. Listening without interrupting honors the speaker. Wait until the speaker is finished. Take a moment to understand what he/she is saying, considering both levels of communication, before answering. Give time for wisdom to speak back. Love never fails. Good communication skills display both love and honor.

How to Repent & Apologize for Hurting Another's Heart

(The How-To of opening the heart for communication)

Preliminary Heart Preparation

1. Begin by first asking the Holy Spirit to help you (see Rom. 8:26.) He will arrange the right time for you to begin. Ask Him also to prepare the other's heart to receive your repentance. Make sure the other person is ready to listen. Get their permission. Only the words the Spirit provides for you will be heard by the other person. Do *not* attempt this without His assistance! Don't get into your flesh!

2. If the person you are repenting to is your spouse or someone else close to you, try to hold their hands if they will allow you. Remember the Holy Spirit is also helping them. Always make eye contact. There must

be a spirit-to-spirit exchange from your eyes to theirs. The touch from the hands also helps in this exchange. Ask, "Will you allow me to repent to you?"

3. Don't give reasons why you have offended the other person or make excuses. Simply admit that you understand that you have hurt their heart. Don't begin with, "*If* I have hurt you..." You are there because you have! Never repent tritely. Give it the same degree of importance as you give to your relationship with the other person. Communicate sincerity.

The 4 Steps Necessary in Repenting to Another's Heart

1. You must convince the other person that you understand the issue and can see that you have hurt their heart. Don't defend yourself or your actions! Say something like: "I can see that I have hurt your heart by..."

2. You must convince the other person that their heart is very valuable to you. Explain how much and why! Say something like: "I want you to know that your heart is very precious to me, because it is who you really are and I do love you."

3. Seek their forgiveness by asking: "Can you find it in your heart to forgive me?" Wait for an answer. However, if you do not receive a positive response or any at all, move forward. Don't feel rejected at this point. Give the Holy Spirit time to soften them.

4. Convince the other person that you have a plan not to repeat the hurt, with God's help. Tell them what it

is! Say something like: "With the help of the Holy Spirit, I plan never to repeat this again. I am aware of what I have done to hurt you and I'm going to take the necessary steps to stop this, including prayer.

Note: When I first learned this heart exercise, in the beginning I had to repent two or three times a day. Each time I was sincere. Each time it became easier, until finally we were both okay with the past hurts.

Principles of Covenant Life

(to be discussed in home groups for practical application)

1. We have moral choices put before us on a daily basis. The same two trees of choice exist today: life or death; blessing or curse; self-centered or God-centered. Choose Jesus! What struggle can you overcome today?

2. Your immorality will overshadow all of your accomplishments. Is this what you want to be remembered for?

3. You also have two choices in this life on earth: humility or humiliation. To be humble is a choice and if not chosen, humiliation will result by default. Which do you most often choose?

4. We must be covered by the blood of our covenant. Without being covered by the blood of Jesus, you are a "dead man walking."

5. The devil is not impressed that we *have* a covenant, but is only defeated if we know how to *enforce* and *apply* the power of the blood.

6. The wages of sin is death. The blood of Jesus brings life and washes the sin away. When the "accuser" reminds you of your sin, remind him of the blood. When your "adversary" reminds you of your past, remind him of his future! Did you know that you have overcome by the power of His blood, and the word of your testimony? (see Rev. 12:11)

7. All the fruit of the tree of the knowledge of good and evil is rotten. Repentance for eating of it will

take its yoke and burden from you before it further goes to seed.

8. A half truth, or a partial truth, is a whole lie. The only absolute truth comes from the Word of God. Are you speaking it?

9. We must take accountability of our own "stuff" and behavior. If you have a problem, don't blame someone else. That's pride; repent! While you point your finger at someone, three fingers are pointing back at you. Don't play the blame game.

10. Obedience keeps peace and order in the Kingdom of God; delayed obedience or partial obedience is called disobedience. It gives birth to the spirit of rebellion, which brings fear and chaos and fuels the kingdom of darkness by means of control and manipulation.

11. Sin is not who we *are*, but what we *do*. God can separate the sinner from the sin. In other words, He separates the person from the behavior! We too must separate the human *being* from the human "doing". This is the basis for unconditional "agape love." Our love must focus on who a person is, not on what he does!

Questions for Further Thought

1. Judging by your past and current behavior, is your life self-centered or God-centered? _____
What changes will you make to have a more God-centered life?_____

_____

_____

2. How accountable are you? Do you accept responsibility for your attitude and behavior or do you pass the buck? _____ What will you do to become more accountable?_____

_____

_____

Prayer

(Repeat this prayer out loud and/or add your own when led)

Come Holy Spirit, help me pray!

Heavenly Father, I give You all glory and thanks for Your Word. I thank You for loving me and sending Your Son. Father, I need You to put Your arms around me now. I believe You'll never let me go and never leave me.

Jesus, I choose to eat of You. You are my "tree of life." Jesus, I receive the life that is in Your blood today by the power of the Holy Spirit. It is You who covers me with Your blood and protects me.

Lord, I thank You for forgiving me of all my sins. I repent for_____(sin)_____. And Lord I forgive all those who have offended me_____(names)_____. I ask You to forgive them also, Father.

Holy Spirit I need Your help. I give You permission to bring conviction to me each and every time I sin, and help me have a spirit of humility and forgiveness in obedience to Your conviction and Word.

I thank You, Jesus, that You have given us power over sin and death by your blood. Thank You, Lord, for restoring my identity, my destiny, and my dominion.

I will believe Your report. I am healed; I am filled; I am free! I refuse to believe any other report. I grant authority to no one else but You!

Teach me how to enforce the provisions of our covenant in the face of the enemy. I will hit him with Your Word.

I thank You, Lord, that You have not given me a spirit of fear, but a spirit of love, strength, and a sound mind.

Jesus, in Your Name, by Your blood and by the power of the Holy Spirit, every generational curse over me, over my spouse and over my family, those I see ____(name)____ and those I can't see, has been broken. Continue to show me where I am no longer walking cursed but subject to Your blessing. I thank You, Lord, for all Your blessings. Amen.

Chapter 3

The Noahic Covenant: God's Family Insurance Plan

✥✥✥✥

"Somewhere over the rainbow, skies are blue."

Adam and Eve were removed from the garden of Eden and the presence of God as a consequence of their sin, but they were not left without hope! As in the verse from the popular song above, they still had a song in their heart put their by their Creator. The covenant promise God made to them, to be redeemed one day by the One coming of her Seed, gave them hope of glory restored and a reason to go on living.

Now, however, begins the long and winding road that leads man back to the heart of God, a road paved with hardship, thorns and thistles, toil, sweat and tears. The promise of something better in the future moves them forward with every beat of their heart. Without that hope, man would surely perish.

After my second divorce there were times I felt so "nowhere" and didn't know why I should even go through the motions of life's daily routines. I felt like an alien on planet earth. But there was that "something" that kept me getting up every morning, shaving, eating, going to work and the like even when my heart felt the paralysis of loneliness and abandonment. Why should I feel abandoned when it was always I who was leaving? Something was still moving me towards tomorrow. Something or someone that moves the creation towards life; some favor, some power, something I hadn't earned, some hope, inspired me and gave me the ability to go forward.

Alienation Propagating

The anguish of alienation from God, from Eden and from life in the Spirit, together with the physical pain and suffering of life outside the garden, were new experiences Adam and Eve had never dreamed of. God's Word continued to move on faithfully even as man began to multiply. Unfortunately, the fruit of sin also multiplied, bringing with it further alienation. Now we find brother killing brother, the alienation of man from man. After Cain killed Abel, the blood of Abel cried out to God for help! Slowly but surely, without its divine love-connection, man's heart was decaying!

50

*Then the Lord saw that the wickedness of man was great in the earth, and that **every intent** of the thoughts of his heart was only evil continually. And the Lord was **sorry** that He had made man on the earth, and he was **grieved** in His **heart.** So the Lord said, " I will destroy man whom I have created from the face of the earth, both man and beast, creeping thing and birds of the air, for I am sorry that I have made them." **But** Noah found grace in the eyes of the Lord...Noah was a just man, perfect in his generations. Noah walked with God.* (Genesis 6:5-9 emphasis added).

The Lord was struggling within His Spirit whether or not He was going to destroy all of His creation. What made Him decide not to destroy all men and beasts? Because He was subject to His own Word given in the Adamic covenant. He remembered His promise to send the Seed. With no man alive, how could He send the Seed? The character and Word of God proved faithful once again. Once God speaks His Word, it must come to pass.

Noah, Mankind's New Hope

God told Noah to build an ark for a big flood that was coming upon the earth to destroy all flesh. He also said to Noah, "But I will establish My *covenant* with you; and you shall go into the ark—you, your sons, your wife, and your sons' wives with you" (Gen. 6:18 emphasis added). This is the first time the word covenant appears in the Bible, but as we have seen, the spirit of this word and its principles were already in effect, even though it as yet had no name.

There are many lessons to be learned here. God told Noah to build an ark for a flood. Can you imagine what Noah thought when he first heard that strange request? If God had asked him, "Have you ever heard of a flood?" he might have replied, "No, uh!" If God had asked, "Do you know what an ark is?" he might have answered, "No, uh!" (Hmmm...I wonder if that's how he got his name!) Just kidding! But how many times does God speak to us in a similar fashion and we think, "My, that's a strange request"?

Why would God's instructions have seemed strange to Noah? Because up to this time it had never rained! The water came up from the ground. So a flood was never even a thought. Noah was to build an ark, never before conceived, for a flood never before experienced!

Noah had to exercise faith in the Word and character of God in order to obey and do this odd thing. Imagine what his friends would say and the questions they would ask him about building that ark! Imagine the ridicule! Imagine the perseverance he had to have building an ark this size for this purpose, no matter what other people said, for the length of time it took him to do it. God was rebuilding the character of man through Noah, or to coin a word, "care-*ark*-ter"! Noah passed the test of obedience that Adam had failed.

What about you? Did you pass the test of obedience! Are you passing it today? Are you committed to pay this price for your relationship with God or with your spouse? Do you have that much faith, trust and patience?

Noah and his household, along with all the animals, over which they had dominion, plus sufficient food for all, entered the ark as God commanded. The ark was built according to the blueprints given by God for maximum protection and efficiency! Notice that the ark now contained the Seed of the covenant that would be carried in one of Noah's sons. This ark, for purpose of illustration, could be called an "ark of the covenant."

Noah passed the test of obedience that Adam had failed.

The Flood

Then came the great flood! It rained for forty days and nights and the waters prevailed on the earth for one hundred and fifty days. Every living thing with the breath of the spirit of life died, *except* those in the ark. The day is approaching when a great spiritual flood will sweep the earth in the last days. Is your ark ready? Are you in covenant relationship with the only true God that will protect you and your family? Genesis 6:22 says that Noah did according to all that God had commanded him. Have you? Have I?

God's New Promise to all Mankind

After the flood, the earth dried out and everybody came out of the ark. God renewed His original Edenic plan and told Noah and his family to abound, to be fruitful, and to again multiply on the earth. The Bible says that Noah built an altar to the Lord and offered animals as burnt sacrifices in thanksgiving for being spared. This blood sacrifice pleased the Lord and He said in His heart:

> *I will never again curse the ground for man's sake, although the imagination of man's* **heart** *is* **evil**

*from his youth; nor will I again destroy every living thing as I have done. While the earth remains, seed-time and harvest, cold and heat, winter and summer, and day and night shall **not cease** (Genesis 8:21-22 emphasis added).*

God will continue to provide for man as He gives him a new start. However, evil still has to be dealt with in man's heart from conception to old age. Seedtime and harvest, sowing and reaping, refer not only to the natural realm but also the heart realm. We have become a product of the seeds we have planted, and are only experiencing the harvest of what we have sown.

What a scary thought! Do you mean to tell me that my first two marriage relationships were simply the harvest of what I planted? *That's* the ship I put my family on to protect them from the flood? No wonder it never survived the tsunami! We all need an ark to protect our family. The only "ship" that can protect our family from impending disaster is a covenant relation-"ship."

Covenant

In Chapter 9 of Genesis God makes the covenant with Noah. The provisions and terms of the Noahic covenant were much the same as the Edenic and Adamic covenants. But in this covenant we see for the first time a *sign* as testimony to the covenant:

*And God said: "This is the **sign** of the covenant which I make between Me and you, and every living creature that is with you, for perpetual generations: I* set My **rainbow** in the cloud, and it shall be for the sign of the covenant between me and the earth...the waters shall never again become a flood to destroy all flesh" (Genesis 9:12-15).

"Somewhere Over the Rainbow" is one of my favorite songs. Who among us has never heard that song or seen *The Wizard of Oz*, the movie classic that made it a hit? The late Judy Garland sang it as no one else could. Ms. Garland, of course, played the role of Dorothy, a young woman lost in a strange land and trying to find her way home. She hears of a marvelous wizard in the "emerald city" of Oz who may be able to help her. She sets off on the yellow brick road to find the wizard and along the way meets up with a trio of odd characters. *Freeze frame!*

Déjà vu? Does that sound like a familiar circular path to nowhere? Are there any "Dorothys" out there who are lost, unsure of your destiny and walking around in a fantasy world dreaming of a person who can give you answers to all of life's questions? Maybe you thought you found such a person, only to discover that he or she was a fraud; just another human being with little power, who had no more idea where they were going than you did. This kind of thing happens every day in the world's dating game.

If you are with a person who is lost and he is your designated leader, where do you think you will end up? If he didn't have a vision, or a plan, or at least a set of blue prints before you agreed to jointly begin life's journey, why did you jump in for the ride? If you don't know where you are going, how will you know when you have arrived? If you don't *know where*, you will be *nowhere*.

Most people in this lifetime have no clue who they really are, much less where they are headed. Unless we understand what our real purpose is on earth, why would any trip anywhere, anytime, for any reason, make any sense at all? Maybe you just like tripping. What if the earthly assignment you are working on turns out to be the wrong assignment? What if your inheritance had been sent to you and you were on the wrong street, on the wrong day at the right time?

I hope you are not one of many today from the tribe of Dorothy. The greatest problem on earth today is ignorance. That was Dorothy's second biggest problem. Her biggest problem was taking the road of ultimate fantasy instead of the road of ultimate reality. She thought she needed help from the wizard of Oz instead of the wisdom of God.

People all over the world are looking and searching for something "out there," maybe even something at the end of the rainbow, only to experience frustration when they can't find answers to their heart's cry. They need to find the manufacturer of all hearts, Jesus. Only then will they be complete and feel fulfilled in this life called time.

Which of the main characters from *The Wizard of Oz* do you identify with and relate to the most? Which one speaks to your deepest heart need?

First, there's the "Cowardly Lion." The lion wanted *courage*. He suffered constantly from *fear*. Obviously, he didn't have a good sense of identity as the King of Beasts. As the top of the food chain he didn't know who he was.

56

As a scaredy-cat he couldn't fulfill his *purpose*. What he really lacked was faith in his real identity.

Then there's the "Tin Man," who needed a *heart*. Everybody needs a new heart and the only person who can give it to us is Jesus. He doesn't even require trade-ins. The "Tin Man" needed a ticker, a spirit mind, a center of his very being. He needed a new anointing, not just an oil can.

Third is the "Scarecrow," who was looking for a *brain*. He thought intelligence was the key to life. He wanted more information. He wanted *brain power*; the power to be like a real human being with all the potential of a man. What he really needed was *wisdom*, the principal thing.

Finally, we come to "Dorothy," who only wanted to find her way *home*. How does she return to the real center of reality? She fell out of *position*. She lost her destiny and her *original source* of provision.

Dorothy eventually made it home, but sadly, Judy Garland never found her heart's true song. Sometimes the lives of movie characters are a caricature of mankind. Each character in *The Wizard of Oz* felt like he or she was lacking something or another. Anyone who is without Jesus will also experience a spirit of lack. In Jesus we are made complete, lacking nothing and having everything, including a brand new heart, a brand new spirit, a purpose and a destiny, along with the power to always feel at home. Remember, Dorothy always had the power to go home. All she had to do was to click the heels of her ruby slippers together. It's truly a pity that so many people today don't know how to access home.

No matter how often I see a rainbow, that awesome sign of God's covenant promise, something in my heart always leaps with joy and hope, reminding me of my relationship with my heavenly Father.

We have witnessed some very deep feelings and sentiments expressed by God. We're getting to know Him and His character and personality more and more. This helps define for us who He is and, therefore, who we are *in* Him. God's Spirit felt sorrow and was grieved. These emotions are part of the cost and risk we must consider to be involved in any relationship. We have seen how one man who walks with God in obedience and by faith can affect many generations to come. Noah heard from God and thereby knew his purpose and destiny, which revealed a vision, which led to the fulfillment of his dreams. He was equipped with all the potential to carry out his instructions from God. Do you suppose this master carpenter's skills were passed down to another famous Carpenter we all know? Little by little this famous Carpenter, by His greatest tool, called the Word of God, can rebuild man. Even if you feel like Humpty Dumpty, Jesus can put you back together again.

Noah responded responsibly to the Word of God. Inside the ark, Noah carried the destiny of the entire human race.

> By **faith** Noah, being divinely warned of **things not yet seen**, moved with godly fear, prepared an ark for the saving of his household, by which he condemned the world and became heir of the righteousness which is according to faith (Hebrews 11:7).

The Seed moves on and the promise continues with the covenant sign for skies to be blue somewhere over the rainbow!

Incidentally, the power that moves us in hope forward through life's obstacle course is *grace*, not a pair of ruby slippers. Grace is what Noah discovered and what every person on earth has access to. Grace is a free gift contained and inherent in the Word of God that offers us His ability and His likeness to keep us on course.

Principles of Covenant Life

(to be discussed in home groups for practical application)

1. Character and relationships are not built in a day. Like the ark, they are built over a long period of time so they are strong enough for any storm.

2. Obedience to God's Word forges the iron of our character.

3. Immaturity is the distance between our word and our character.

4. Faith is the substance of the things hoped for, the evidence of things not seen (Heb. 11:1). It is a pre-requisite to be in covenant relationship with God

5. God's protection always comes with His covenant. As long as we are in the ark, we will be protected from the rest of the world. There is no protection, however, when we jump ship; relation-ship, that is!

6. Our covenant also protects our children, their wives, and their children. This is the best family insurance plan God offers.

7. Men, are you getting the message as the covenant initiator of your household? You must be sure that all your household is in your ark. For them to be protected, you must be under the authority of God's Word, or you have no ark.

8. What friends and family say about our calling and hearing from God cannot keep us from pounding nails. We must be willing to build our ark without their help.

9. Covenant promise casts out fear. If the radio says, "A worldwide flood is coming that may destroy the earth," why are we not afraid? Knowledge of and faith in every word and promise of covenant will always bring us peace.

10. Every Word that proceeds from the mouth of God is a rainbow!

Questions for Further Thought

1. How would your family members or closest friends describe your character?_____
_____If immaturity is the distance between our word and our character, how mature are you? _____
_____

2. Covenant promise casts out fear. Are you walking in fear or in faith? _____ If fear, what will you do to start walking by faith? _____
_____
_____

Prayer

(Repeat this prayer out loud and/or add your own when led)

Come Holy Spirit, guide me as I pray!

Heavenly Father I thank you for sending Your Word to me today! I plant it deep inside of my heart. I, too, am grateful that I have found favor from You, as did Noah. I can walk with You as he did. I can hear from

You as he did. Holy Spirit, anoint my ears to hear every Word from my Father, and anoint my feet to always walk in His paths.

Father, I thank You for forgiving me from every evil intent of the thoughts of my heart. Jesus, I thank You for Your blood that washes the sin from my heart, especially_____(sin)_____. Thank You Lord!

Holy Spirit, I cherish a spirit of obedience to Your every request, no matter how strange it may sound. Continue teaching me to walk by faith, and not by sight.

Lord, Your heart is so valuable to me, help me to be sensitive not to hurt others' hearts either, especially my spouse ___(name) ____. Help my eyes to see and my ears to hear my spouse's heart, and all those in my household.

I thank You for revealing more of Yourself through Your Word. I love You for who You are.

Holy Spirit, I give You permission to continue molding me and fashioning me in the character of Jesus Christ, my Savior. You are the potter and I am the clay.

Lord, thank You for Your covenant protection over me and my family! Teach me how to remain always under that protection in obedience and faith.

Lord, I will not walk in fear in these evil days, but in the strength of our covenant. Every time I see a rainbow and the splendor of its color, I will remember You and Your love and all Your promises to me and mankind! Thank You for this confidence and blessed assurance! Amen.

Chapter 4

The Abrahamic Covenant: Cutting a Blood Covenant

How are you doing so far? Are you getting the message that God speaks to the man first and calls him to be the leader of the household? Pick out some of the foundational principles of our faith in this chapter and continue building your understanding of relationship. The Seed moves on in the bloodline of Noah through his son, Shem. Eventually, through the genealogy of Shem, comes Terah, who begot Abram, around the year 2000 B.C (see Gen. 11:10-26).

Have you noticed? God's ways and time schedule are quite different from ours, aren't they? God is so patient to carry out His redemptive plan. Or maybe it is we who are slow to obey and are holding it up. Either way, man doesn't look like he's responding well to God's agenda. Who will teach man that God wants things done decently and in an orderly manner in order to accomplish His Will? Obviously, man needs help, but who is able? After the "Tower of Babel" episode (see Gen. 11:1-9), humans will have difficulty even in communicating with each other. Help!

The Creator Himself is the *only* one able and qualified to rescue His creation. Since His product is malfunctioning, the Manufacturer will have to come back on the scene for some technical adjustments. He's going to show man "one more time" how it's done! Man is going to learn covenant relationship if God has to educate him in person!

> *Now the Lord had said to Abram: "Get out of your country, from your family and from your father's house, to a land that I will show you. I will make you a great **nation**; I will bless you and make your name great; and you shall be a **blessing**. I will bless those who bless you, and I will curse him who curses you; and **in you all** the families of the earth shall be blessed"* (Genesis 12:1-3 emphasis added).

The last verse contains the promise, *in you*, the reference to the Seed and the word *all*, referring to both Jews and Gentiles. This Seed will be the blessing to all people, no matter what race or color. It includes and is available to everyone. This means you, too! Where Babel divided man into races, the Seed will bring them back together as *one*. Many colors, one rainbow! Even though each man is individually unique, the day is coming when he will share again a common identity as a family and nation. (One blessed nation under God, indivisible, with liberty and justice for all!)

Get out of town! Go to a place where you will no longer depend on your parents. Trust God when He tells you to leave to a place He sends you. He wants to be your source, wants to talk with you there, provide for you there and wants your undivided attention away from all the distractions and familiarity of your "old" home neighborhood. There is where you will grow up, and fast. There is where your inheritance will be, in the land to which he sends you. Don't try to go back. It'll never be the same again. Yes, it will be a test of faith. It won't be easy, but it's the price of growing up.

After God had given to Abram and all his descendants forever all the land that he had seen, He said,

> *"Look now toward heaven, and count the stars if you are able to number them." And He said to him, "So shall your descendants be." And he believed in the Lord, and He accounted it to him for righteousness* (Genesis 15:5-6).

So by faith and belief in God and His Word, Abram was declared righteous and became the father of a great *nation* known as *Israel.*

The Blood Covenant

Let's take a break for a bit and look at more history of covenant. In the ancient Eastern culture two men would "cut" a covenant in the following manner. Before they made their vows to each other, they would cut or split a bull or another animal in half and spill its blood in sacrifice. They would then separate the two pieces and pass between them. Upon completing this, they would make their oath in the presence of a witness, who was usually a priest. Whatever they promised to each other was then considered sacred and binding unto death.

The essence of the words they exchanged was, "All I have (my possessions such as land, wealth, food, house and the like) and all I am are yours" (my very life is at stake here). They agreed they would rather suffer the same fate as the animal they sacrificed than to ever break this blood covenant! The penalty for breaking their oath, by actions contrary to their words of promise, was death to the party who violated the conditions set forth in the covenant. Death was the only means by which one no longer was held accountable to his vows. Death, however, did fully satisfy the promise.

In a similar manner God "cut" a blood covenant with Abram and showed him how to do it:

> *So He said to him, "Bring me a three-year-old heifer, a three-year-old female goat, a three-year-old ram, a turtle dove, and a pigeon." Then he brought all these to Him and cut them in two, down the middle, and placed each piece opposite each other...Now when the sun was going down, a deep sleep fell upon Abram...And it came to pass, when the sun went down and it was dark, that behold, there appeared a smoking oven and a burning torch that passed between those pieces. On the same day the Lord*

made a covenant with Abram, saying: "To your descendants I have given this land, from the river of Egypt to the great river, the River Euphrates— (Genesis 15:9-18).

The smoking oven and the burning torch were the two parties that *passed over* the blood between the pieces of the sacrificed animals. This was a vision of the Father and the Son making the covenant agreement on behalf of all mankind. All man had to do was rest (or, literally, sleep), because one day Jesus would take man's place and satisfy all the covenant requirements for man, including giving His life. All man has to do, then, is to receive that covenant by faith and believe it. Man didn't have to earn it by his works or performance. Jesus cut the covenant. It was a free gift to us from Jesus. Don't you just love Him?

A Carnal Plan

Now Abram was eighty-five years old and Sarai, his wife, was in her seventies, when a carnal plan for children popped up in her mind. By her own reasoning and impatience, and the fact she was past child-bearing age and barren, she made a choice to see to it that they would have a child. She confronted Abram with a plan for him to have sex with her maidservant, Hagar, the first surrogate mother-to-be. This plan, same then as now, was and is not God's plan. (Does this scenario resemble the choice their ancestors made back in Eden?)

How often, after hearing from God, do we come up with our own plan instead of waiting for God's Word to become manifest in our lives? The consequences for any carnal plan cannot be measured at the time. The victim, as always, is the innocent new born baby; in this circumstance, Ishmael. Because this plan was not carried out according to what God had purposed, and was therefore a sin of disobedience, its results badly missed the mark. It affected not only Ishmael, Hagar, Abram, Sarai, and all their descendants, but also all those still living in the Middle East today. One degree off of God's plan can have devastating effects. Who's to blame? It was man's choice. The wrong tree was selected again, along with its rotten fruit.

Abraham, the Father of Many Nations

God returned to the scene thirteen years later, when Abram was ninety-nine years old. God, the covenant initiator who knows all, talked with Abram saying: "As for Me, behold, My covenant is with you, and you shall be a father of many nations" (Gen. 17:4). Notice closely what God says here. Hagar was an Egyptian. After the Tower of Babel, the family of Ham was dispersed into many lands, including Egypt. In all likelihood, Hagar was a descendent of Ham. God takes into account the Ishmael factor, which represented now more people of promise and He says, "No longer shall your name be called Abram (*exalted father*), but your name shall be Abraham (*Abra-Ham*); for I have made you a father of many nations" (Gen. 17:5). This is good news for all who thought they had no biblical ancestry. When God makes a covenant with you, your identity and destiny change!

> *And I will establish My covenant between Me and you and your descendants after you in their generations,*

70

*for an **everlasting** covenant, to be God to you and your descendants after you* (Genesis 17:7 emphasis added).

The word "everlasting," in God's terms, means for eternity or eternally (as is His Word). Can you believe your eyes and ears? An eternal promise from God to be their God has been given to all who receive this covenant and believe! This means you, too! When you're in covenant

When God makes a covenant with you, your identity and destiny change!

with Him, a dramatic change occurs in you, which brings with it the promise of your eternal destiny. And He will never break it.

Sign of the Covenant

Now comes the *sign* of the covenant, as was the rainbow for Noah:

This is My covenant which you shall keep, between Me and you and your descendants after you: Every male child among you shall be circumcised; and you shall be circumcised in the flesh of your foreskins, and it shall be a sign of the covenant between Me and you (Genesis 17:10-11).

The cutting away of the flesh, which caused blood to be shed, was the outward sign of covenant. The symbolism of circumcision is death to the flesh and dying to self. What is meant here by the word flesh is that part of man's fallen nature that must be cut off. We need to die to self if we are to have any relationship in the proper order. Circumcision was an outward sign of the covenant, but it didn't necessarily include a change of heart. For any relationship to change it must take place on the inside; be accompanied by a change of heart with its corresponding change in one's belief system.

"Is there anything too hard for the Lord?"

No matter what your past track record says, God can author a complete restoration of your heart if you allow Him to and believe His Word. This story continues with God telling Abraham that by Sarah (changed from Sarai, by covenant, to mean "princess"), he will have a son. Abraham fell on his face and laughed (holy laughter). He was one hundred years old and Sarah was ninety! Imagine if this happened to you or to your grandparents at that age! Grandpa, what a man! Grandma, the poor little thing! But how could this be? This doesn't make any logical sense!

How often are we faced with an unseen, invisible, impossible situation like this that appears to make no sense? For example, "Will I ever be able to recover from that past relationship?" Could you believe God when your mind says, "No way"? Your attitude instead should be, "Never mind what circumstances, appearances or people might indicate; what did God say?" Sometimes we have to laugh at our circumstances and the way God handles them. Abraham laughed in faith but Sarah laughed in unbelief. Wouldn't you laugh too? Or cry? Their son Isaac was born, nonetheless, just as God had said, and his name means "laughter". "Is there anything too hard for the Lord?" (Gen. 18:14) Nope!

It is interesting to note that here, during this episode of the promise of the birth of Isaac, is the first appearance of the covenant meal. After a covenant was cut, the covenant partners sat down together and shared a meal to celebrate the event in appreciation of all that had happened and been promised.

> *Then the Lord appeared to him by the terebinth trees of Mamre... "And I will bring a morsel of bread, that you may refresh your hearts..." So he took butter and milk and the calf which he had prepared, and sat it before them; and he stood by them...as they ate* (Genesis 18:1-8 emphasis added)

Can you picture this meal? Imagine that you had invited God Himself to sit at your table to wine and dine. Would it refresh your heart as you broke the bread? Would you put on a banquet for the Lord? How would you look? How would you prepare your house for this romantic interlude? Candlelight? The best wine? The fatted calf? How would you act if the King showed up? Would you truly honor Him? Let's make it even better! What if He invited you? That's what can take place each time we share Holy Communion at His table in His house! I'm sure that in that instance, every breaking of the bread and drinking of the wine with Him would improve your relationship.

Why not also treat your spouse that way at each meal? I'm also convinced it would spice up your marriage and enhance the romance if you would treat your spouse with that same honor. This is what happened that day as a standard to celebrate with your loved one all that you have promised in your covenant vows.

Covenant

Another manner of cutting a blood covenant was for two persons to cut their wrists and commingle the blood by pressing the open wounds together. This was a common practice in the history of the Native American Indian. In other places around the globe, such as Africa, we still find people today making oaths by commingling their blood and even by drinking it. To a Westerner who's not familiar with the origin of this ritual, it does sound a bit bizarre. Remember, however, that throughout the eastern cultures people believed the "life" was in the blood. The sentiment of all and the words they spoke from their hearts were in essence the same as above. A sign, mark (such as a scar on the wrist), or something of value was exchanged representing this sacred event. The penalty, likewise, was always death for the covenant breaker.

Archives show there have been various types of covenants, but the three most common ones made are for the following:

1. *Protection:* e.g. tribe A, a weaker party, seeks to covenant with tribe B, a strong warring tribe, for protection against all enemies that would hinder their lifestyle.

2. *Business:* e.g. tribe A, an agricultural people, seeks to covenant with tribe B, a seafaring tribe, to exchange their commodities for improving their overall health and diet.

3. *Love:* e.g. party A, usually a stronger party, seeks to covenant with tribe B, a weaker party, for the sheer purpose of *blessing* the other. *Marriage* is a love covenant!

Marriage, a Love Covenant

Let's briefly sum up some covenant components we have studied so far to the extent that they relate to your marriage love covenant. Consider anything that is out of order, which you might want to realign.

1. Your covenant marriage continues daily in the presence of God the King as if you were in Eden, and is therefore considered holy ground. You acknowledge daily that you are subject to the authority of every Word of the King. The High Priest, Jesus, is your witness, as are the angels and saints along with the others in attendance.

2. The husband, the stronger and more responsible party, the covenant initiator, continues to bless, honor and protect his wife, the weaker party. (He is only stronger if he has a right relationship with God in the role for which God gives him strength to carry out His purpose.)

3. The husband determines to bless his wife daily from a heart of unconditional love as his vows stated: "I take this person, for better or worse, for richer or for poorer, in sickness and in health, to love and to cherish from this day forward 'til death do us part." This is based on who she is and not on what she

75

does. *According to his vows, he is committed unto death; divorce is **not** an option.*

4. The weaker party (in role order only) receives this promise and exchanges her vows with the same words. (She is the covenant partner and submits to the authority of God given to the man, and where she's weak, God then becomes strong in her.)

5. These vows that have been exchanged are unbreakable, irrevocable, and your very lives depend on keeping them as you have stated.

6. Your hearts have expressed "All I am and all I have are yours!" (Can you see why prenuptial agreements do not qualify as a love covenant?)

7. Rings are exchanged as signs to remember this event every time one looks upon them. They are placed on the ring finger that is directly attached to one's heart beat.

8. The marriage covenant meal is celebrated with Holy Communion. The body and blood of Jesus ratify the covenant with a banquet to follow.

9. Sex is the sign of the celebration of the love covenant completed. Marriage was designed by God for a male and female, both being virgins, to leave their parents (who are God's agents) and cleave to each other. The man enters the woman, thereby breaking her hymen, causing her blood to flow upon him, and physically consummates their marriage covenant by becoming one flesh! More important, however, is the spiritual union created when their hearts are in one accord, which surpasses the physical realm, especially when for physical reasons this could not be

possible. All deviations to God's design are regarded as abuse to the human product and will result in malfunction.

10. Now two, single, whole persons become one, a brand new identity functioning as a family unit. One new relationship, yet retaining each person's uniqueness. God's spiritual mathematics, one male plus one female = one. No exceptions to this equation are allowed. Not to be divided but multiplied.

Your covenant marriage continues daily in the presence of God the King as if you were in Eden, and is therefore considered holy ground.

Well, that was almost brief!

Marriage Problems Arise

Since we have just mentioned marriage as a love covenant, let's get back to the story and take a look at some of Abraham's marriage problems. Chapter 12 of Genesis reveals a flaw of character in Abram. When Abram went down to Egypt to sojourn there, before entering he said to Sarai his wife:

> Indeed I know that you are a woman of beautiful countenance. Therefore it will happen, when the Egyptians see you, that they will say, 'This is his wife'; and they will kill me, but they will let you live. Please say that you are my sister, that it may go well for my sake, and that I may live because of you (Genesis 12:11-13).

What's wrong with this scenario? In the face of adversity, the covenant initiator should have been willing to lay down *his* life, not offer hers. The real issue here is, "Will it be her life or mine?" The relational message he sent to her heart was that her life was not as valuable or as high a priority as his. Her protector cowered. Don't you think this would be an excellent time for repentance?

This same flaw shows up again in chapter 20:

> *And Abraham journeyed from there to the South, and dwelt between Kadesh and Shur, and stayed in Gerar. Now Abraham said of Sarah his wife, "She is my sister." And Abimelech king of Gerar sent and took Sarah* (Genesis 20:1-2).

He did it again! Can you believe it? Many times we push family members aside for our own selfishness. So many times we make promises to our children to take them somewhere fun and instead go to the office. Have you ever had to wait for a parent who never showed up? How did you feel? Does your relationship suffer a setback when they do not keep their word? Always consider this as a heart issue regarding spouses and children! Especially, fathers and husbands, as the stronger party it is your overall responsibility to protect their hearts.

Fortunately for Abraham, Sarah and all of mankind, God stepped in and spoke to Abimelech before another seed and its consequences had to be dealt with. (The First Covenant Initiator is always responsible for our protection.) If you read further, however, this iniquity was passed on to his son Isaac, who did the same thing with his wife Rebekah and with Abimelech the king (see Gen. 26:1-11).

This kind of thing can become a *generational iniquity*; some call it a curse. The iniquity of the father gets passed down as in "Like father, like son." This has to be dealt with sooner or later, but man doesn't know how to stop this pattern from entering into his marriage relationship or keep it from his children. There seems to be an unseen law or principle operating here that man is helpless in stopping. It is called the *law of sin and death*. Man can't stop it without help (see Rom. 7:1-25).

Giving Your Favorite Possession to God

Now came still a further and uncompromising test of Abraham's faith. After waiting until he was one hundred years old for a son, he finally begot Isaac. Truly he was a proud father. I'm sure he took him fishing, taught him everything about farming and animals, showed him all about life and all the stories and experiences he had witnessed. You can bet Abraham spoiled his only son and invested a lot of time and love in him. Imagine the lessons Isaac was taught about God, family, kings, land, wells, Egypt, Sodom and Gomorrah, geography, history, etc.! Then, when he was a well-trained youth and a most vital part of the family, God spoke this to Abraham:

> *Take now your son, your only son Isaac, whom you love, and go to the land of Moriah, and offer him there as a burnt offering on one of the mountains of which I shall tell you* (Genesis 22:2).

How many different thoughts and alternatives must have gone through his mind? God will always stre-e-e-e-e-e-e-e-e-etch our faith! "Just what is faith?" you might ask. "Now faith is the substance of things hoped for, the evidence of things not seen" (Heb. 11:1). Faith is the functional prerequisite to our relationship with God and with each other. We grow in faith with our obedience to every Word that proceeds out of His mouth. "Without faith it is impossible to please Him, for he who comes to God must believe that He is, and that He is a rewarder of those who diligently seek Him" (Heb. 11:6).

> *Faith is the functional prerequisite to our relationship with God and with each other.*

Take a look now at the covenant relationship picture the Bible is about to sketch for us. It is a shadow or forerunner of the heart attitude and substance of things hoped for and the prophetic evidence of things not yet seen but which are to come. I will put in parentheses, next to the following scenes in Genesis 22, the preview of the coming Seed and Redeemer, Jesus Christ, God's perfect blood covenant:

Abraham, the father of many nations, took his only son, Isaac, whom he loved (as did God, the Father of all creation, give His only Son, Jesus) to offer him as a blood sacrifice on a mountain (to offer Him as a Blood Sacrifice on Calvary).

> *So Abraham rose early in the morning and saddled his donkey,* (as Jesus rode the donkey into Jerusalem. See Zech. 9:9 and Matt. 21:4-5)...*So Abraham took the wood of the burnt offering and laid it on Isaac his son;* (so also they made Jesus carry the wood of His cross)...*Then [Isaac] said, "Look, the fire and the wood, but where is the lamb for the*

burnt offering? And Abraham said, "My son, God will provide for Himself the lamb for a burnt offering." (Jesus was to be the Lamb of God that was to be offered as a sacrifice for our sins. See John 1:29)...*and he bound Isaac his son and laid him on the altar, upon the wood."* (So also they bound and nailed Jesus to the cross at the altar of Calvary.) *And Abraham stretched out his hand and took out his knife to slay his son. But the Angel of the Lord* (the Lord Himself) *called to him from heaven..."Do not lay your hand on the lad, or do anything to him; for I know that you fear God, since you have not withheld your son, your only son, from Me...blessing I will bless you, and multiplying I will multiply your descendants as the stars of the heaven and as the sand which is on the seashore; and your descendants shall possess the gate of their enemies. In your seed all the nations of the earth shall be blessed, because you have obeyed my voice."* (this seed will be one day the Seed, Jesus, who will crush all enemies.) (Genesis 22:3-18).

Jehovah Jireh, Our Provider, will provide our Lamb!

How must Abraham have felt on the way up the hill to kill his only son? His heart must have been pounding so hard that it felt like it was going to break! Contemplate the tears of love and sorrow that must have run down his face as he clutched the knife! I'm sure the heated emotions of the moment were more than overwhelming. Would you be able to do anything like this with any one of your children after raising them from conception and loving them with your whole heart? You would rather rip out your own heart! Better yet, you'd rather exchange your life for any one of theirs. Well this is exactly how God the Father felt as He observed this scene! He knew the pain, since this is what He had already decided to do with His Son, Jesus Christ. Is this love? You tell me!

Abraham Passed the Covenant Test

Abraham passed the test of obedience and faith in the Word of God. He had an "inner image" of what it takes to be willing to give "all you have, and all that you are", as a covenant partner. He was willing to relinquish his most valuable possession, or "darling", his very son Isaac, for the sake of this relationship with God. When our tests come, are we going to be able to trust in His Word? In the face of financial hardship will we trust God for provision no matter the circumstances? During sickness, disease, or a doctor's report that we are going to die, who's report will we believe?

When your job fails, your relationships are going south, and even your marriage feels hopeless, can you stand on His Word? Will you be able to bring your most valuable possession to the altar to Him? How about your children, your grandchildren, your spouse, your job, anything else that comes before Him…including yourself? Are you willing to wait for an Isaac experience, or in haste do you have a tendency to settle for an Ishmael experience—the wrong car, the wrong job, the wrong purchase, the wrong choice in a marriage partner—and suffer the consequences? Be willing to wait on God for the revelation marriage partner that He brings to you. Deny any carnal plan.

It will affect your destiny. You are the sum total of your choices and life's decisions, because as a man thinketh in his heart so is he. Be led by the Spirit before making any decision of consequence.

In Isaac the seed moves on through his son Jacob, who is to be called Israel, and Jacob's twelve sons, who are to be the twelve tribes of Israel. The covenant continues on in them. Our knowledge of His ways and of His thoughts also progresses with the infusing of the Abrahamic Covenant.

Blood Covenant Blessings

By now you are beginning to understand the vital importance of having blood covenant as the cultural backdrop of an entire nation. God put covenant into man's culture so that when it is in place it will insure that man will be *blessed* every moment of his existence. God is love, and love manifested is called *blessing*. In other words, the very nature of God as Love and as our love covenant initiator necessitates His desire to bless all of creation at all times. Love without blessing is not love. Its very essence requires sharing and giving.

The Trinity is the most perfect example of this love shared in God in the relationship of the Father, Son, and Holy Spirit. God is always positioned to pour out His blessings upon us! However, we are not always positioned to receive all He has for us. Man limits God's blessings because the condition of his heart prevents him from receiving them. God has always promoted His ways, His thoughts, His will, His Word, His purpose, and His kingdom. God's transmission is always going out but the problem is with the ears of the receiver. God has chosen to operate only in light and there is no darkness in Him. When we choose the wrong tree or the wrong kingdom of darkness, we automatically cut ourselves off from receiving His blessings.

The purpose of blessings is to multiply and prosper us, to impart our true identity, to empower us to reach our destiny, to exercise our true dominion and potential, and to fulfill our purpose for being created. There is a scheme, however, as we have already stated, that breaks the flow of these blessings and power. This scheme is to prevent the heart of man from receiving the love of God and His blessings and instead receive hurt which hardens the heart and cuts him off from his source of life.

In America today, the critical times in life for us to be blessed and thereby have our heart protected according to God's plan have been literally ripped out of our culture along with all the safeguards that have been removed. As God's covenant rebuilders, we are determined to put them back into place and restore those "old paths, where the good way is, and walk in it; then you will find rest for your souls" (Jer. 6:16). We are further determined to "build the old waste places...raise up the foundations of many generations...be called the Repairer of the Breach, the Restorer of Streets to dwell in" (Is. 58:12).

The Seven Critical Times of Blessing

I would like to share with you one of the greatest revelations I have had while putting my life, marriage and family back together. This is what every man and every church should be practicing. Let's take a look at God's original

84

blueprint for blessing man found within His old covenant relationship with us, where He put into the ancient Hebrew culture the protective measures to insure His blessings during seven critical times in an individual's life-time. (Remember the principle, "you can't *cleave* if you don't *leave*," and blessing releases you to leave! God designed us to go from one critical time to the next blessed: from blessing to blessing and from glory to glory!) The seven critical times of blessing are at or during the following times:

1. **Blessed at Conception.** When your conception was blessed your spirit felt wanted, accepted and received. By design, however, this blessing can only occur between two people (parents—male and female) in a covenant marriage relationship. It must occur in love and not in lust. Otherwise, a curse results leaving the child's heart feeling unwanted, rejected and resented. The ancient Jews took this very seriously. Deuteronomy 23:2 stipulates that no person of illegitimate birth or their descendants to the tenth generation could "enter the assembly of the Lord." Some of the potential consequences for a child conceived and born outside of wedlock or in lust are feelings of rejection, depression, fear, lust, irrational anger, guilt, and shame. "I didn't ask to be born" or "I'm a mistake." In Old Testament law, the penalty for fornication or adultery was death. In ancient Hebrew culture children were considered a blessing from God and marriage was held in high reverence.

2. **Blessed during Pregnancy.** When blessing came during your mother's pregnancy, again you felt

85

wanted, accepted and received. There was little emotional stress and turmoil and you received much nurturing, love and affection. A curse brought opposite conditions and the same feelings as those in a cursed conception. Psalm 58:3 says: "The wicked are estranged from the womb; they go astray as soon as they are born, speaking lies." God's provision was that the mother was relieved of all other duties during pregnancy and there was a healthy cultural attitude towards children. Pregnancy was an honor, not a burden. Parents would even speak to the baby in the womb and tell the baby how much they loved him/her.

3. **Blessed at Birth.** When a birth was blessed, the child was received as the gender God created and was nurtured and loved by the parents. There was a reasonably trauma-free birth. If cursed, the child was born the wrong gender (according to the parents) was neither received nor loved, and often had trauma during birth. The potential heart results for the child were feelings of fear of death, insecurity, fear in adulthood, homosexuality, striving to become what the parents wanted and anger and frustration. The entire community anticipated the birth of a child with joy. In accordance with God's plan, on the eighth day after birth male children were blessed by the rabbi, circumcised and named.

4. **Blessed during Infancy.** If you were blessed during infancy you had the feeling of acceptance, love and nurturing. You were breast-fed and shared a close bonding with your mother. You also had the physical

affection and touch of the father. However, when cursed, you were deprived of these things; little or no bonding occurred and your security needs were not met. This further resulted potentially in fear of death, difficulty in establishing a self-identity and the inability to trust others, including the Lord. God's concern for the baby was provided in the mothers' attitudes of making the infant a priority and in the combined cultural attitudes of family and covenant marriage. Already the attitude of the child was formed, and his heart was established by blessing or by the lack of it.

5. **Blessing at Puberty.** At puberty you were blessed in the following manner: the parents separated your identity from your behavior; your relationship with your parents facilitated sharing of feelings and the father through his acceptance and words of blessing severed your identity from your mother. His threefold blessing contained the following:

a. confirmation of your gender identity;

b. confirmation of God's blessing and plan;

c. parental blessing and release into manhood/womanhood.

Puberty could be cursed when the parents cursed your identity in an attempt to correct your behavior, through lack of an open relationship with your father, when there was no acceptance or blessing, through a parental attitude of shame or embarrassment over physical changes and through sexual violation, molestation or incest. The potential heart results were feelings of insecurity and insignificance, striving to prove manhood or womanhood, rebellion, lack of release into proper gender identity, retention of identity with the mother, life-long unrest in the soul and quest for identity. God's plan: Bar Mitzva and other such ceremonies to honor the child now as a young man or woman. Friends, I hope you can see why we have so many of our children in the streets, in gangs, emotionally sick, and doing all these strange behaviors. It's not just being young and dumb; it's from not being blessed properly by the father and mother to put the youth's heart at rest.

6. **Blessed at Marriage.** The marriage was blessed when the son or daughter was blessed by both parents in marriage. The right to make a choice, even if considered wrong, was upheld by the parents. The parents accepted and received the son's or daughter's marriage partner and both sets of parents blessed the marriage. The marriage was cursed when the parents refused to come to the wedding, if they maintained that it was a wrong choice and wouldn't work, if they refused to accept the marriage partner and if they wouldn't release the son or daughter to cleave to the spouse. This curse could potentially result in the marriage laboring under a curse, feelings of judgment, resentment and bitterness toward parents (bondage) and both marriage partners striving to disprove parents. In addition, this unhealthy tie to parents could cause either partner the inability to cleave to their spouse. God's remedy was that marriages were arranged by parents, and thus always blessed. The culture contained covenant understanding of marriage. Parents,

for lack of knowledge, have caused so many heart problems for their married children.

7. **Blessed during older age.** In older age the blessing would come to the parents from their children who would rise up and return their love. This completed the family cycle of blessing and each person would go from glory to glory by design. However, when they were not blessed, the potential results were that the children would curse their parents later in life, the children would be retained in bondage and never come to know Christ (the imperfect ending to the scheme), the parents might never come to know Christ and the parents might be robbed of enjoying their children's friendship. Under this curse children might never be blessed and freed into their identities. Their lives might be shortened and unprosperous due to dishonor. In the ancient Hebrew culture God saw to it that children would honor and highly esteem their parents. The parental blessing of children created a desire to bless the parents and promoted its generational continuation.[1]

The Good News

The good news is that because we can receive the blood of Jesus Christ today, we can apply it to all those critical times when we were cursed rather than blessed and be free! We simply have to be led by the Holy Spirit to repent of our unforgiveness of all those who have cursed us and

---

1. The information on the seven critical times of blessing were taken by permission from the teaching material of a "Curse to Blessing Seminar" by Family Foundations International, Pastor Craig Hill, Littleton Colorado.

forgive them. Because of Jesus' death, burial and resurrection, His blood heals our heart and breaks these curses, which in most cases were generational patterns. Then we need to thank our heavenly Father for His blessings, making sure our heart before we ask His blessing. Otherwise, it will not happen.

The Real Life Example of our Youngest Son

As I'm sure you know, over half of marriage relationships today end in divorce and my wife and I were once part of those staggering statistics. Just what happens to all those who have been divorced? Is there any hope for them? We would like to share with you the following actual scenario that took place before we were married in blood covenant, and how things dramatically changed after the blood covenant was in place. Our son has agreed to allow us to use him in this example.

The good news is that because we can receive the blood of Jesus Christ today, we can apply it to all those critical times when we were cursed rather than blessed and be free!

Before I met my wife, she already had two children. When we decided to marry the first time, we didn't know any of these principles mentioned above. However, lack of knowledge did not excuse us from the consequences of failing to apply them. They applied even if we were not aware of them. Watch how this life drama unfolds when we don't do things according to God's ways.

90

First, we were in rebellion for simply being divorced and remarrying. We didn't even know what the word rebellion meant at the time. We though it was par for the day. The three year old boy who became mine in our marriage was conceived out of wedlock. He was not my biological son but I became his father nonetheless. Of course, the child is always the innocent victim of the parents' lawlessness. His conception was not blessed. She wasn't married to the biological father and so the conception by default was not in love. A great start for this young spirit, wasn't it? It progressively gets worse from here.

During her pregnancy her fear and the tension between her and the baby's father were received by the infant in her womb, reconfirming his feelings of not being wanted or accepted. The pregnancy was very difficult and traumatic and the mother was sick nearly the entire term; she even became dehydrated. By the time the child was born his spirit sensed something was wrong but of course could not verbalize it. To make matters worse, the father claimed the child wasn't even his. This added to the child further insecurity and the striving to be loved at an early age.

When I came on the scene, I didn't have a clue what this child was feeling inside and now, to make matters worse, he had to accept another man as his dad after having lived a short time with his biological father. It pains my heart now to understand the burden this little boy was carrying in his young life. To add insult to injury, not only did he carry the iniquities of the first father, but here I came with a shopping list of my own, including rebellion and lust, since his mother and I were "living together" before we decided to marry. What a great covering I've provided! Now he's living under the roof of a rebellious father who has separated himself from any blessing from God because of his own lawlessness! It was the spirit of "stupid" gone to seed. Does this in any way resemble a "covenant initiator"?

Then, at puberty, when he really needed a blessing from his "father," his mother and I got divorced! Incidentally, this is when most divorces occur, just when the oldest child needs the puberty blessing. It's a great scheme of the devil to get the man out of the house so he could plunder it (see Mt. 12:29). How could he possibly have any sense of identity, or sense of purpose, or sense of anything at all? Now that I was out of the picture, the forces of darkness came in like a thief. I left the "door open" because where I was supposed to be the "strong man" of my house, I was bound up. I gave the authority to Satan and his scheme to steal, kill and destroy our son.

He soon left home on his own, as many young men do, to live with his friends and run the streets.

How foolish the statement is, "Why are the kids today so rebellious"? Why do you think they get into gangs? Why do they start substance abuse? Why sex, drugs and rock and roll? Simple: we bought them tickets in the front row and led them there. We put them on a one-way track with a one-way ticket. They're out there looking for purpose, identity and blessing. They try to get love from anyone out there. There is only one way back, and it's by a Savior and Redeemer, Jesus Christ!

Our son became a substance abuser and was dying. He and his friends went from one house to the next until they wore out their mother's welcome and patience. They would sleep during the day while the parents worked and go out into the night after having emptied the refrigerators. His mood swings went from one extreme to the other. He was struggling to hold onto life but he couldn't stand in quicksand. To further complicate his life, he fathered a daughter out of wedlock, true to the generational pattern he was subject to, but couldn't manage the responsibility to help her or her mother because he couldn't help himself. (She is absolutely precious! God is taking care of her and her mother most lovingly.)

Two years after his mother and I were divorced, God miraculously put us back together by the power of His Holy Spirit. We were drawn to a divine appointment with each other and our Maker by Our Heavenly Father. One night we attended a Christian seminar called "From Curses to Blessings" by our new pastor, Craig Hill, mentioned above.

Were we prime candidates for that seminar or what! There was such a strong anointing on that seminar that we repented to each other and to our God and the reconciliation and restoration process of our marriage relationship began. The Holy Spirit came upon us, melted our hearts and led us into repentance and forgiveness. Not only did He save us from ourselves as we were spiraling downward after each of us had a brush with death, we were now going to be remarried in a "Blood Covenant."

To be remarried after divorce to the same person would have to be either a miracle or a bomb! One victory after another came into our lives. Next, the very thing we abused, marriage itself, was going to be our ministry and testimony. But what about the children! What about our son, still in Egypt? Even though God had forgiven us and blessed us, the consequences for our son were still in effect. I want to tell you today that your blood covenant with God includes your children. Even if they are not yours by your blood, they are provided for by His Blood.

In His perfect timing and heart preparation, the Holy Spirit arranged a showdown with destiny between me and our son, on behalf of Our Father, who wanted to bless us. We had so many angry flesh confrontations prior to this day, that I had to pray even to be able to look at him. His irrational anger for me as the authority figure had been bottled up in him since his conception. Someone was going to pay for this injustice done to him. Not knowing any better, or that Jesus had already paid for these things, he held me responsible for the tremendous hurt stored up in his heart.

I was downstairs one night and heard him come into the house. As usual, I didn't want to see him or to deal with his drunkenness. As she always did, my wife had prayed the night before that he would get his life back in order and be delivered from all of his oppression. As a prayer warrior she also prayed that he and I be reconciled. True to His Word and His promise in Malachi 4:6: "And he will turn the hearts of the fathers to the children, and the hearts of the children to their fathers"…it happened!

I came upstairs at my wife's insistence to find my son crying uncontrollably. I thought he was just "high" again on drugs, so at first I had no compassion. That's how strained our relationship was. My wife looked at me because she sensed in the Spirit what needed to happen. She prayed in the Spirit as hard as she could. The moment of truth had arrived. The thought crossed my mind that I was not going to repent to him, even though I knew these principles, because my flesh wanted to react as I had trained it to do. The Holy

Spirit put a tug of conviction on my heart to obey now; I would never have another opportunity like this again.

I obeyed and the Spirit helped me through the following anointed dialogue by His power as I said, "I have hurt you son, haven't I? You're very mad at me, aren't you? You're mad at me for leaving you and divorcing your mother, aren't you?" He then cried even worse. I said, "Son, I was wrong and I hurt you so much, and you didn't deserve any of what you had to go through. This is all my fault and I have sinned against you. Could you find it in your heart to forgive me?"

He wept more and could hardly speak as he sobbed between each word he tried to utter. Finally he said, "Dad, you were my hero. You were my hero, and you hurt me so much." I held him tight and he held me also. It was a moment of love so intimate that we had needed so badly but had been too paralyzed with anger to express. I said, "Son, I love you and I am proud to be your father and for you to be my son."

That was what he had wanted to hear since conception. Those were the words he had needed to hear in his spirit from me on behalf of His heavenly Father. He got his Father's blessing through me and it put to rest the torment and void his heart had carried up to that hour. His countenance changed and life came back into his face. The same Holy Spirit had come upon him and begun his restoration.

I had another opportunity to bless my son at a Promise Keepers meeting in Mile High Stadium, Denver, Colorado. I invited him to come with me that weekend. He told me that he felt that God was cleansing him from his sin. The Holy Spirit was speaking to me about unconditional love.

It was time. We went into our R.V. with about five friends as witnesses. Again, I got down on my knees and told my son "I am so proud of you." I repented and promised in front of God and these witnesses that I would never again withdraw my love from him due to his behavior. I said, "I choose to love you no matter what your behavior. Good or bad, I will always love you. Will you forgive me for withdrawing my love in the past?" He answered, "yes." Afterward, we hugged and talked together as if nothing had ever happened in the past. God is so awesome!

Today he is a Spirit-filled, tongue-talking Christian. He has completed his military obligation with the U.S. Army and has recently come home after serving one year in Iraq. Currently, he is married and going through the post-war adjustment period. The process God started in him will be completed in due season. This we know. Today he is blessed and it has been prophesied that he will one day join up with our ministry by the blood of the Lamb and with the word of his testimony!

Dads, moms, this restoration of blessing is available to you too in blood covenant!

The Story of the "Monkey Trap"

While I was serving in the U.S. Army in Vietnam, I learned a valuable parable. The Vietnamese had an ingenious way to catch monkeys. They would take a coconut and cut a hole just big enough for the monkey to squeeze his hand into. Then they would put small rocks into the hole for the monkey to grab onto. The monkey's curiosity at the sound the rocks made inside the coconut caused it to reach in and grab the rocks, making a fist around them. The curious, stubborn monkey would not let go of those rocks and its fist was too large to fit through the hole. That monkey was determined to hang on to its newly-found treasure no matter what the consequences. The hunters, seeing the monkey "holding on" to what was going to prevent him from climbing any tree to escape, proceeded to chase him down. "Holding on" to this "thing" cost the monkey its life.

Moral: Anything you are "holding on" to from the past and just can't seem to let go, could result in your death, both physically and emotionally. If you are willing to let it go; if you believe that Jesus has already done something about the way you feel by His death, burial and resurrection, release it *now*! Let it go before you lose your life over it. This applies to anything that comes between your heart and God, even if it is a person such as your "Isaac." It's *idolatry*! Bring it to the altar! Let it go! Don't monkey around with it!

Principles of Covenant Life

(to be discussed in home groups for practical application)

1. Abraham is called the "father of faith." Since we are the "seed" of Abraham, just how do we, his children, execute faith? First, we must have the same object and substance to believe upon and hope for that Abraham had. This, of course, is the Person, character, and Word of God Himself. He is the "Rock" upon which we stand. Faith comes into our h-e-a-r-t by what we h-e-a-r.

2. The Covenant Initiator is ultimately responsible for teaching and maintaining the principles of covenant relationship in his generation, family, and culture for its future continuation. This secures identity, destiny, purpose, vision, and potential for those descendants that follow, provided that each generation chooses to do the same.

3. God will sometimes move you away from your kindred and send you to a new land for your spiritual upbringing and ultimate good. Your separation will teach you to become utterly dependent upon Him. There, you will be taught to walk by faith and learn to hear His voice. In the land or place to which He chooses to send you, you will experience your greatest anointing, grace and blessings and the power to fulfill His will. This is a divine appointment. Don't miss it!

4. God has only one plan for you—His! When first we hear it, we tend to come up with our own. These carnal plans have serious consequences. This is just

98

another manifestation of rebellion and disobedience. Repent and ask forgiveness.

5. As the text mentioned, we must be circumcised as the sign of our covenant with God. We know now that it is the flesh attitude in our heart that must be "cut off" on the inside.

6. Faith is saying yes to God, no matter what the appearance of the situation, circumstance, or condition. If God says it, it becomes possible! The power, potential and possibility are in the Word. We therefore do not walk by sight or by emotion but by faith planted in our heart from hearing this Word.

7. Your faith will always be tested, no matter your age! As gold, we too must go through fire so that all the dross is removed. He is the Potter and we are the clay to be transformed.

8. Any idol you are clinging to, whether a person, place or thing, must be let go. God is a jealous God. In our relationship with Him, He will allow no other gods before Him.

9. He is *mono-g-am-ous! One-God- the I Am- to us.*

Questions for Further Thought

1. If you are the husband, how do you honestly measure up as the covenant initiator in your marriage?_____

What do you need to do to improve in this role?

_____

If you are the wife, how supportive are you of your

husband in this role?_____

How can you be more supportive? _____

_____

2. As the "seed" of Abraham, in whom or what are you
   putting your trust? Are you trusting in God or in the
   things and ways of the world? _____

   What do you need to do to trust God more fully?

   _____

   _____

Prayer

(Repeat this prayer out loud and/or add your own when led)

Holy Spirit, please help me change my heart!

Lord, thank You for Your Word. Thank You for giving me the gift of faith. Thank You for being a holy,
true and faithful God in whom I can put my faith.
My trust is in You. My hope is in You. You are the
substance of my heart. You are my evidence of all
the things not seen. With You, nothing is impossible. You are everything to me. Without You, there is
nothing. You are my source and my God.

Holy Spirit, continue teaching me to walk by faith in
Your ways and Your thoughts. For Your thoughts
are higher than my thoughts and Your ways higher
than my ways.

Plant Your Word deep inside of me, to the very depth
of my heart. Renew my spirit mind. You have created in me a new heart, Oh God. I gave my old heart to

you in exchange for Yours, one that can see as You see and hear as You hear, and love as You love!

Thank You for forgiving me, Father, of all my unbelief and disobedience. Please take away all the dross from my heart as You mold me and fashion me according to Your Will.

I repent for all idolatry, especially_____ (name)_____. I confess it as sin. I lay it down before Your Cross, Jesus. Wash me with Your Blood, and cleanse me from this spirit of idolatry and defilement. Your blood makes me without spot or blemish in our relationship. Holy Spirit, lead me not into temptation but deliver me from this evil.

I thank You for circumcising the flesh from my heart with Your Word, the two-edged sword. Cut away all that is carnal. I agree with Your Plan for my life.

Finally, Lord, I desire to be called a man/woman of faith. I desire to leave all those who follow after me with the legacy of faith and the knowledge of You and the Blood Covenant. I will bless and be a blessing according to Your Word. I thank You today for all of my blessings and all those You have brought unto me to receive Your blessings!

Abraham was called the "father of our faith," but You, God, are the "Father of all faith." We, Your children, thank You! Amen!

Chapter 5

The Mosaic and Palestinian Covenants: Laws of Love

※ੴ◆ﭨﭕ

I n your family, in your marriage, in your home, in your heart, which is more abundant: love or law? Which rules? Would you agree that the more love you have, the fewer rules you need to make? And would you also agree that the less love you have demonstrated in your home, the more rules you have to enforce?

How did your first child react to the word "no" or "not"? How do we still respond to these words? Something inside of man doesn't like the "n" word! How many times did you have to use it in training your children? How is it progressing today when the "n" word is given in a command or even a request?

Adam and Eve did not respond well to the one directive they were told *not* to do. Their display of disobedience resulted in a flaw of character, called an iniquity, and that is what we have inherited from our first parents. When we are told "no," even if we accept the instruction, there is a tug of rebellion to that authority. Gentlemen, when she said "no" on your first date, how did you react? Was it because you were not really a gentleman? Ladies, is it difficult for you to say "no" to him and "yes" to God so that you will remain a lady? Never mind the first date. How are you handling "no" today in your relationship with God and in your marriage?

Love and law; can they coexist? Not only can they, but they must, in order to pass the test of faith in and obedience to the Word of God. Law is certainly not the goal of relationship but the laws are necessary for the lawless. Love is the goal of *all* relationships of value. It should be the beginning, the means and the end of every relationship. Does this sound familiar? The Alpha, the Way, Omega, and Creator! Whoops! Too Soon! Got carried away!

In addition, marriage should not be your ultimate goal but the means towards the ultimate end: love. As we stated earlier, "Beloved, let us love one another, for love is of God; and everyone who loves is born of God and knows God. He who does not love does not know God, for *God is love*" (1 Jn. 4:7-8). Just to jog your memory, isn't this why you are taking this journey? As soon as this goal is reached and is in place, seldom do laws have to be enforced. They will be in place in your behavior and in your actions as the fruit of the love you have in your heart. Perfect love needs no laws imposed from without.

Since we cannot reach that level by ourselves, which position only God Himself occupies, we need them! God, our Maker, understands His product much better than the product understands itself. Until *Marriage should not be your ultimate goal but the means towards the ultimate end: love.* we die to self, and thereby can cheerfully take "no" for an answer, we need laws, both spiritual and natural. The purpose for laws is order. The law of love brings order to our heart. I must remind you that spiritual laws are higher than natural laws, because what is seen was created by the unseen on this scene.

The Ten Commandments

The Ten Commandments are the laws God first gave us through Moses. God gave mankind a set of laws that were designed to help reprogram man's "temporarily out-of-order" heart. They are a part of the covenant He gave to Moses for all of mankind. Ever since God issued them in 1445 B.C. they have been controversial and misunderstood and remain a contentious item today. Let's take a look at some scenes from the desert experience of Moses and the children of Israel. Grab something to drink! This chapter can be very hot and dry; might even make you uncomfortable.

In real life, every love story has its wilderness experience. Every ministry will have to spend time in the desert classroom away from the comforts of home. Why? It's time to grow up! Hopefully, you'll never have to spend forty years taking laps around Mount Sinai getting your heart right before you cross over the Jordan River into your promised land!

Over four hundred years after the Abrahamic covenant, God called Moses, a type of savior of his people, to leadership over the twelve tribes of Israel. For most of his young life Moses had been used to living in the luxury of Egypt as a royal prince. He later fled Egypt as a fugitive for murdering an Egyptian. By God's hand, Moses came back to Egypt forty years later to lead about three million people, the children of Israel, out of slavery in Egypt under Pharaoh Rameses II, and into the wilderness.

From riches to rags, from comfort to the wilderness, I know the feeling all too well. This has happened to me twice! The first time, I was yanked from my comfortable college life with all its youthful pomp and circumstance and given a 2-year full scholarship, including room and board, that was sponsored by the U. S. Army. If that wasn't a culture shock, the one-year expense-paid vacation to the Republic of Vietnam was. I had to leave my country, my family, my house, my friends and my classic, custom 1950 Chevy 2-door coupe behind. In an all but friendly manner they took my clothes, my Nikes, my hair and my collegiate athletic reputation and gave me some ugly green clothes, heavy green boots and a nasty hair-cut. They even put my name on dog tags. Dog tags! Does that tell you something about how I was going to be treated?

My fourteen-month stay in Southeast Asia lacked the allure and glamour of a Caribbean cruise. There were times Vietnam was so hot it was hard to catch your breath. My job title was what they called a "grunt." Boy, what *that* word did for my sense of identity and worth! A grunt was the term for an infantry, walk-everywhere soldier. I walked through some desert land, walked, or I should say tripped, through some triple-canopy jungle, and walked through many rice paddies. I had to walk everywhere and put many miles on my boot odometer. It was truly a wilderness experience for me. I wasn't fed manna but C-rations and a meal called "lurps." I don't know how to spell that word because I didn't even know what it was. It tasted like, "What is this?" I'll tell you more about that adventure later on in the book.

The second time, I was doing quite well financially, living in Denver, Colorado, with the green and sometimes snow-covered backdrop of the beautiful Rocky Mountains, when one day my wife and I were sent by God to the western plains of Kansas. Believe me, it was not only a shock from our former comfort, but also required an adjustment from big city life to rural, agricultural, small-town life. Where are the restaurants? What do you mean, "We only have a Dairy Queen?" I look back now and have finally figured out why God has to take us out of our comfort zones. He wants to get our total attention without distractions. It worked for me and it worked for Moses and the children of Israel. Got to admit God chooses some strange locations to set up His classroom for training us! That must be where the military got its idea.

After God had parted the Red Sea so that they might cross over, Moses and the Israelites came months later to the wilderness of the Desert of Sinai and camped there before the mountain. Don't you find it interesting that the war in Iraq has been staged in the same arena and location where the Israelites walked for forty years? Here are some of the highlights of Moses' experience.

> *And Moses went up to God, and the Lord called to him from the mountain, saying, "Thus you shall say to the house of Jacob, and tell the children of Israel: 'You have seen what I did to the Egyptians, and how I bore you on eagles' wings and brought you to Myself. Now therefore, **if you will indeed obey My voice and keep My covenant, then you shall be a special treasure to Me above all people**; for all the earth is Mine. And **you shall be to Me a kingdom of priests and a holy nation.**' These are the words which you shall speak to the children of Israel"* (Exodus 19:3-6 emphasis added).

Abraham's covenant was still in effect when this Mosaic Covenant at Sinai was given with the following conditions: "*If you will obey...then you shall be...*" Father God is the teacher of how they should conduct themselves. They are to be a "*kingdom of priests and a holy nation.*" In other words, given their new identity, that is how they will exercise dominion, keeping in mind of course, they are still under the authority of "*the King.*" The word "holy" means set apart, dedicated only to Him, and not belonging to the secular world. An entire kingdom of priests, holy unto Him, is to be literally His government on earth! More identity! Further potential! Clearer Destiny!

They answered, "All the Lord has spoken we will do" (Ex. 19:8). Right! Obedience to the Word of the King was again essential for the relationship to be fulfilled, practiced, and to function best for the good of man.

Why did God give man a list of ten commandments? Do you recall when man first ate the fruit of the belief system of the kingdom of darkness? That fruit didn't go into his stomach. It went straight to his heart. Man was given a new programming designed to delete the old system. When God wrote His instructions upon the two new hard discs in tablet form it was intended to update the new heart computer. To re-program, all man had to do was obey. Incidentally, these commandments were chosen precisely to identify and correct the exact opposite thinking and behavior that man currently was practicing. Here are the "Ten Commandments" as they came to Moses after thunderings, lightning, a thick cloud on Mount Sinai that completely covered it like smoke from a furnace (because the Lord descended upon it in His covenant fashion) and a trumpet blast that got louder and louder:

And the Lord spoke all these words, saying:

"I am the Lord Your God, who brought you out of the land of Egypt, out of the house of bondage.

"You shall have no other gods before Me.

"You shall not make for yourself a carved image— any likeness of anything that is in heaven above, or that is in the earth beneath, or that is in the water under the earth; you shall not bow down to them nor serve them. For I, the Lord your God, am a jealous God, visiting the iniquity of the fathers on the third and fourth generations of those who hate Me, but

109

showing mercy to thousands, to those who love Me and keep My commandments. (This heart program replaced the idolatry currently in practice, and if obeyed would correct the heart's plumb-line and restore north to man's compass.)

"You shall not take the name of the Lord your God in vain, for the Lord will not hold him guiltless who takes his name in vain. (They lacked reverence and honor for His name. That kills all relationships.)

"Remember the Sabbath day, to keep it holy. Six days you shall labor and do all your work, but the seventh day is the Sabbath of the Lord your God. In it you shall do no work: you, nor your son, nor your daughter, nor your manservant, nor your maidservant, nor your cattle, nor your stranger who is within your gates. For in six days the Lord made the heavens and the earth, the sea, and all that is in them, and rested the seventh day. Therefore the Lord blessed the Sabbath day and hallowed it. (This heart program was designed to keep the kingdom of God in perspective and a priority over worldly attachments. It guaranteed proper health and strength to the spirit, soul and body.)

"Honor your father and your mother, that your days may be long upon the land which the Lord your God is giving you. (Lack of honor for Father God or lacking honor for parents, which is a love choice, shortened not only life's journey, but also affected one's overall prosperity.)

110

"You shall not murder.

"You shall not commit adultery.

"You shall not steal.

"You shall not bear false witness against your neighbor.

"You shall not covet your neighbor's house; you shall not covet your neighbor's wife, nor his male servant, nor his female servant, nor his ox, nor his donkey, nor anything that is your neighbor's" (Exodus 20:1-17).

These last six reflected lack of love for one's neighbor, not only in actions, but also in thought and word.

The heart manufacturer was delineating the heart manual for the heart's best performance and long life. The commandments reflected the true state of the heart. Man's heart problem had to be addressed. I know you're probably wondering why all these were written out in full! Be honest: for some of you, this is the first time you have

Keeping [Jesus' commandments] should flow effortlessly as our love response to His covenant with us.

really read them in full-scale. Please don't lie; you'll be breaking the ninth one!

My friends, we are still breaking these commandments most the time. The commandment manual just couldn't do the job Emmanuel was to be sent to do. How can we truly say we love Him if we don't attempt to keep these and when some still have no knowledge of them? Jesus said, "If you love Me, keep My commandments" (Jn. 14:15).

Keeping them should flow effortlessly as our love response to His covenant with us.

The Mosaic Blood Covenant

Moses sent young men of the children of Israel to sacrifice peace offerings of oxen to the Lord. Then Moses took that blood and sprinkled it on the altar, which he had made with twelve pillars according to the twelve tribes of Israel. He also sprinkled the people and said, "This is the blood of the covenant which the Lord has made with you according to all these words" (Ex. 24:8).

The Bible says that right after they heard the words of the covenant "...they saw God, and they ate and drank" (Ex. 24:11). That's what it says! They saw God. When you are in covenant relationship you will see God from the eyes of your heart.

The children of Israel then were told to make an ark that contains the Testimony of all the things God gave them in commandment. They carried that ark with the conditional covenant *with* them as they traveled and they also carried the unconditional covenant *in* them. So, the children of Israel were told how to conduct themselves in their personal, social, and religious lives. It went in one ear and out the other, not stopping to stick in the *heart*.

The Threshold Covenant or Covenant of Hospitality

Right after I was married in covenant, I lifted my wife into my arms and carried her over the threshold of the doorway of our house. Do you know where that tradition began? If you haven't experienced that practice or are unaware of its origin, let me explain its genesis. And men, after hearing this explanation, if you haven't done this, maybe you'll consider doing it today. Its practice goes back to the ancient Hebrew culture of *Threshold* Covenant, also called the Covenant of *Hospitality.*

Picture an entire family gathering at an altar in front of the door to their house. (This is still practiced in some eastern cultures.) There they would gather to worship God, putting in place as a result an implied covenant of hospitality to whoever would thereafter enter the door of the house. It was this ritual that blessed the house and blessed every guest who stepped inside the door. In Spain, for example, a remnant of this custom says, "Mi casa es su casa" (My house is your house). Everything in the house was now available to the guest, as if he were a co-owner.

Tradition said that if you enter my house I, the owner, would protect you with my life. Also, after a guest entered into your house, he could not be harmed while inside. A good example of this traditional practice can be found in the Scriptures when Lot invited the two angels into his house and would not allow the intruders to enter and carnally have their way with the two guests (see Gen. 19:1-8). Lot would not permit them to be harmed as long as they were under the shadow of his roof. Even today, if you enter a house in some of the Eastern cultures and remark how much you like a certain article in that house, it will be given to you.

At the threshold of the door was a little basin called a *caph* in Hebrew. Into this *caph* (pronounced sawf) they would pour out the blood of a dove, pigeon, lamb, ox, or fatted calf. People would use the blood of the animal they could best afford. The more valuable the guest was, the more valuable the animal that was to be sacrificed. The blood of the fatted calf was the most valuable and was poured into the *caph* before royalty, such as the king, would enter the house. The blood represented the very *life* of the host. The greatest insult to the owner was to refuse to enter and pass over the blood, the owner's life, or to step in the basin or trample the blood underfoot (see Heb. 10:26-29).

My wife and my family never seemed to bond. Because she was my second wife, she never felt accepted by my side of the family. There was always tension in her heart when they had to fraternize or intermingle. This went on for more than twelve years. When I finally carried my bride over the threshold and my right foot first touched down on the other side, she immediately felt officially adopted into the family. She now knew the covenant meaning of crossing over the threshold. Something broke on the inside that day and this simple execution and its understanding had settled her heart's concern.

This tradition has the husband presenting his bride to all his family as an expression of honor and acceptance into the household. Basically, by my doing this I was announcing, "She is now bone of my bones and flesh of my flesh and I will protect her with my life!" The issue was settled and her heart felt welcome. It no longer mattered what they all felt or would say. The only thing that mattered was what my actions affirmed.

There was another traditional custom for a king in regards to his relationship with his loyal subjects in reference to this threshold covenant of hospitality. Since there was no modern technology for communication, the king would have to visit his subjects in person. The king would travel about his kingdom in a caravan, led by his army, to see who was loyal to his reign. The people would take some hyssop, or use their hand, and dip it into the blood of the *caph* and put it above their doorposts to display their loyalty. If the king saw the blood, he knew he was welcome, would then enter and say, "I will be your king and you will be my people." If there was no blood on the doorposts, the king would send his army in to destroy all those not pledging their obedience to him!

The Jewish Passover

Now that we understand the threshold covenant, let's take a closer look at the most obvious example of one in the Old Testament: the Passover. First let me explain another Hebrew word: *pacach* (pronounced paw-sakh'), which means to cross over, pass over, covenant cross or enter into covenant. *Pacach* is the Hebrew verb used in Exodus 12:13 and 12:23 to paint the picture of the crossing over of the threshold and thereby entering into blood covenant. This is its only meaning in the Hebrew language and can be found only in one other place in the Bible. The problem we have had lies in the English translation of Passover to mean skip over or spare. We therefore have been limited in our understanding of the real picture and meaning because we were taught over the years the English translation. The noun in Hebrew for the Passover is *Pecach* (pronounced peh'sakh) closely resembling the verb, *pacach.*

115

We've understood Passover, symbolically in the natural, to be a festival delineated in detail to Moses by God. It was to be celebrated by the congregation of Israel by taking a lamb "without blemish" and after killing it, taking the blood and putting it on the two door posts and on the lintel of the houses where they would eat it. The Lord's Passover was a day they were to keep as a memorial for all generations as a feast by an everlasting ordinance. It takes place every year in remembrance of the night the final plague came against the firstborn of Egypt. It was the day judgment was executed upon all the gods of Egypt but the Israelites were not harmed. It marked the day they were brought out of the land of Egypt. And so, we have thus believed.

However, there was a greater occurrence that day in the spiritual realm that accounted for these things to happen. When the unseen King passed through the land, He was looking for all those loyal to His kingdom. As was the custom, all those loyal would put blood on their doors, so the king would see the blood from afar and would not send the army in to destroy them. The key was the blood at the threshold of the entry of each dwelling. It meant the King was welcome to enter into the house and even was welcome to sit down and have a meal with them, and break the bread:

> *Now the blood shall be a sign for you on the houses where you are. And when I see the blood, I will pass over (pacach) you; and the plague shall not be on you to destroy you when I strike the land of Egypt* (Exodus 12:13).

God was saying He was going to pass over the blood at the door and enter into each house at their invitation as a reconfirmation of their covenant relationship with Him as He covenant crossed spiritually in the tradition of blood covenant.

Again, in Exodus 12:22-23:

You shall take a bunch of hyssop, dip it in the blood that is in the basin (caph), and strike the lintel and the two doorposts with the blood that is in the basin. And none of you shall go out of the door of this house until morning. For the Lord will pass through to strike the Egyptians; and when He sees the blood on the lintel and on the top of the doorposts, the Lord will pass over (pacach) the door and not allow the destroyer to come into your houses to strike you.

Now that the invisible King was present, who was in fact the Covenant Initiator, He would also be their Protector from any harm! Praise the Lord for the true revelation of Passover!

What did this mean to me? Back to the time I was serving in Vietnam. The truth is every day I had fear that I was going to die. In my heart I believed that death was on its way and it was just a matter of time before I had to look death in the eye and accept it. I could feel it approaching me as each day dawned. At every sound of a sniper's bullet, at every explosion of a land mine, and upon every enemy attack and fire fight, I got myself prepared to die.

Quite often we would gather together at night to chat about home, home cooking and all the other good things in the U.S.A. A group of us would share our philosophy of life and expound on the reality of our circumstance. We asked things like, "What are we doing here?" or "Will I make it home?" or "What will I do if my leg gets blown off?" or "Is there a God?" or "If there is a God, who is he?" In our group were a few believers as well as some non-believers, including an agnostic and an atheist. We all shared one common sentiment: fear.

One night after asking these same questions and always searching for the answers to soothe our fear, at least temporarily, something amazing took place. It was somewhere between two and three o'clock in the morning. I was asleep but was suddenly awakened by a voice in the pitch-black night. It was an authoritative voice, one that not only awakened me from a sound sleep, but also unnerved me. At the sound of the voice I began shaking as it said, "I am Love!" The words were crystal clear, as if someone was standing over me and speaking right into my ear. I looked around to see who it was that spoke these words to me. There was no one there. Perhaps it came from a radio. But it was two in the morning and everyone was sleeping. I thought, "Maybe I was just dreaming."

Now sitting up in bed, I thought I might just as well lie down again, when the same voice again repeated those same words, "I am Love." This time I was awake for sure. My entire body started to shake and tremble, a strange heat filled my body from head to toe, and even the hair on my arms stood up. I knew in my heart of hearts that those words came from God Himself. The reason I immediately knew that it was God was because of the peace and warmth that totally permeated my being. The word "love" then expanded to an illuminated understanding of everything I was searching for in my daily questioning. God had revealed to me in a very real way His bottom line identity, Love.

The next thing I thought was to go and tell my friend, who was also a believer, what had happened to me. As I walked to where he was sleeping, I found it strange that he was on his feet heading towards me. When we were about fifteen feet away from each other, we both simultaneously pointed our index finger at each other and at the same time we said to each other, God is love!" He said, "God just spoke to me." I said, "God just spoke to me too!" He spoke the same thing to both of us. This was the confirmation that this wasn't something imaginative, but real! We hugged each other while dancing around in a circle with joy. Others said, "Hey, keep the noise down. We're trying to sleep. What's wrong with you guys, anyway? Do you know what time it is? Have you guys been smoking pot, or what?" No, we were not drunk as they supposed, just supernaturally high on God.

The Great I Am is Love. It became my entire theology. I heard His voice, felt His presence and received His love. I found out later in a Bible verse that "perfect Love casts out fear." That's who He is and that's what happened. The fear of death left. What had taken place was I finally opened the door of my heart and welcomed the King to enter, so the destroyer, using fear and terror, had to leave. When you ask Jesus, the King, to enter into the door of your heart by the blood, and you believe He shed His blood to wash your sins away, the King will reside in you and protect you from all fear.

The Palestinian Covenant

(Allow me to comment on these verses as I apply this covenant to my life.)

These are the words of the covenant which the Lord commanded Moses to make with the children of Israel in the land of Moab, besides the covenant which He made with them in Horeb. Now Moses called all Israel and said to them: "You have seen all that the Lord did before your eyes in the land of Egypt, to Pharaoh and to all his servants and to all his land—(I have seen and felt the King's hand on me and how He has protected me.)

The great trials which your eyes have seen, the signs, and those great wonders. Yet the Lord has not given you a heart to perceive and eyes to see and ears to hear, to this very day. And I have led you forty years in the wilderness. Your clothes have not worn out on you, and your sandals have not worn out on your feet. (He has been with me throughout my desert experiences. He has clothed me, fed me, and sheltered me no matter the circumstances to this very day in this covenant relationship.)

You have not eaten bread, nor have you drunk wine or similar drink, that you may know that I am the Lord your God. And when you came to this place, Sihon king of Heshbon and Og king of Bashan came out against us to battle, and we conquered them. We took their land and gave it as an inheritance to the Reubenites, to the Gadites, and to half the tribe of

Manasseh. Therefore keep the words of this covenant, and do them, that you may prosper in all that you do (All I have to do is continue believing.)

All of you stand today before the Lord your God: your leaders and your tribes and your elders and your officers, all the men of Israel, your little ones and your wives—also the stranger who is in your camp, from the one who cuts your wood to the one who draws your water—that you may enter into covenant with the Lord your God, and into His oath, which the :Lord your God makes with you today, that He may establish you today as a people for Himself, and that He may be God to you, just as He has spoken to you, and just as He has sworn to your fathers, to Abraham, Isaac, and Jacob. (Nothing has changed. He wants everyone of His family back home.)

I make this covenant and this oath, not with you alone, but with him who stands here with us today before the Lord our God, as well as with him who is not here with us today (Deuteronomy 29:10-15). (This covenant offer is available to anyone who wants to receive it.)

For this commandment which I command you today is not too mysterious for you, nor is it far off. It is not in heaven, that you should say, 'Who will ascend into heaven for us and bring it to us, that we may hear it and do it?' Nor is it beyond the sea, that you should say, 'Who will go over the sea for us and bring it to us, that we may hear it and do it?' But the word is very near you, in your mouth and in your heart, that you

121

may do it. (The covenant is at hand right within your reach in the person of Jesus, the Word.)

See, I have set before you today life and good, death and evil, in that I command you today to love the Lord your God, to walk in His ways, and to keep His commandments, His statutes, and His judgments, that you may live and multiply; and the Lord your God will bless you in the land which you go to possess. But if your heart turns away so that you do not hear, and are drawn away, and worship other gods and serve them, I announce to you today that you shall surely perish; you shall not prolong your days in the land which you cross over the Jordan to go in and possess. I call heaven and earth as witnesses today against you, that I have set before you life and death, blessing and cursing; therefore choose life, that both you and your descendants may live; that you may love the Lord your God, that you may obey His voice, and that you may cling to Him, for He is your life and the length of your days; and that you may dwell in the land which the Lord swore to your fathers, to Abraham, Isaac, and Jacob, to give them (Deuteronomy 30:11-20). (It's simple! It's a matter for all to choose life or death. It's further a matter of eternal life to those who choose to love the Lord and hear His voice.)

The book of Deuteronomy contains in detail the commandments, the statutes, the judgments, the blessings and the curses. There is no mystery in the above verses. They are direct and to the point and lay out a basic and beautiful plan. These passages spell out God's will and purpose for man. Man's response from his *heart* is the keynote issue here. Will these words of God turn the people around? Not yet! They still can't see or hear! Their heart is blind and deaf!

As soon as God made the Mosaic covenant with them, they broke it! They worshiped a golden calf! Whose character, again, was in question here? Obviously God has kept His Word. After Moses returned the second time with the two tablets, and after the sin of the people, God again revealed His commitment to mankind as He revealed His loving, forgiving Nature:

> *The Lord, the Lord God, **merciful** and **gracious**, **longsuffering**, and **abounding** in **goodness** and **truth**, keeping mercy for thousands, **forgiving** iniquity and transgression and sin, by no means clearing the guilty, **visiting** the **iniquity** of the fathers upon the children and the children's children to the third and fourth generation* (Exodus 34:6-7 emphasis added).

And according to this Word, and true to His Nature, He made the Palestinian covenant with this generation, some born after the exodus from Egypt. God's Heart was always right, but man's heart was still stiff-necked and experiencing God's curses and punishment for the consequences of their disobedience. Man still couldn't take "no"!

Man, we just don't get it! The world is in chaos today for the same reason. We just don't listen or obey. The Old Testament word "obey" simply means to believe in the connotation of New Testament meaning. Most of us don't even want to believe all the miracles God performed for the children of Israel in the wilderness or the miracles He is still doing today for his children, the Church. Someone told Kenneth Hagin that it wasn't a miracle that God parted the Red Sea to allow the Israelites to escape the army of Pharaoh. He said his study showed that there is a season when the Red Sea is at low tide and the water is only about a foot deep. "That's really how they crossed. That's no miracle." Kenneth Hagin replied, "Praise God, now that's even a bigger miracle than I ever thought. What an awesome miracle it was, then, for the entire Egyptian army on horses and chariots to drown in one foot of water! Praise God!"

An Illustration of God's Love

A lot of us think, "God doesn't love me because I have disobeyed Him," and "He's mad at me," and "He only loves me when I keep His commandments." That's how we feel. Please take a look at a fictional illustration to clear up this misconception.

Let's say God owns a hot air balloon and He is going to give you a free ride in it with Him. The ride will take you higher than you have ever been, above the clouds, to places you have never seen, to everywhere that is beautiful for as long as you wish the ride to last! He gives you a free ticket for this ride in exchange for your faith. He even gives you a choice whether you want to take this ride or stay behind. He does warn you, however, that once you get in, "Do not jump out while the balloon is in the air. There will be consequences if you do; you will crash and burn! Please don't leave Me while this craft is in flight, because I have to remain with My balloon as its Captain, and I don't want to see anyone get hurt."

He also says that if you stay on board, in the basket, you can become joint owner of the balloon. Now should you choose to ride and give Him your ticket of faith, but decide to jump out while it is in flight and crash and burn, or stay on the ground and not enter, what should be your conclusion? "Well, God just doesn't love me!" Wrong! The balloon is His Kingdom and ways. The conditions of the covenant are not based on God's lack of unconditional love. Rather, they show and give us the free will opportunity to respond from our heart in love to be included in His Kingdom in obedience to the King.

Nothing can separate the King's love from us, but we can choose to separate our love from Him. God's love is never based on what we are doing or what we have failed to do but on who we are in covenant relationship with Him. God can separate our behavior from our identity! The covenant is based on the fact that He desires us to become His children of righteousness in spite of our good works or in spite of our sins.

Parents, do we quit loving our children if they break our rules? We are all aware of how much that hurt us as kids whenever we felt our parents didn't love us. That's where my belief system was off. God unconditionally loved me. My parents have unconditionally loved me. So, why did I go wrong with my family? I withdrew my love from them on occasion because of their bad behavior. My rules failed to demonstrate any love and were perceived to come from a self-righteous tyrant.

There must be still something lacking in the love department of my heart that needs to surface. What's holding it back? The process of renewing my heart with the Word has to run its course, so that at the same time it results in the death of my flesh. My flesh has been crucified with Christ, so now my heart must now believe it is dead and begin to walk in that reality. Thank God, that wasn't His way or attitude towards me.

We can start today and make a decision from our heart to not ever withdraw our love from the person we married and be able to separate their value as a person from their behavior.

Are we able to lovingly discipline our children for their disobedience without shaming their identity? Begin by saying, "What you did was wrong, and that has consequences but I still love you because you are my child."

As covenant husbands and wives we must learn to separate identity from behavior in the same manner. It's paramount to having a healthy relationship. I always remind myself of my wedding vows where I said the words, "*for better or worse.*" These words pertain also to all behavior, better or worse, fighting or loving, yelling or listening, agreeing or disagreeing, right or wrong. We can start today and make a decision from our heart to *not ever withdraw our love* from the person we married and be able to separate their value as a person from their behavior.

Are laws ever going to change our hearts? Obviously not! We are still looking for an answer to the dilemma of the heart condition regarding the children of Israel. The

126

heart is a lonely hunter seeking its salvation but it is not to be found in the Law. What do you think the answer is? When your relationships seem to be going in circles through the desert, what do you do to take yourself out of the tailspin? What's it going to take to put the romance back on track in this unstable love affair and reconcile the way things were back in Eden? The answer is coming! The Seed of that promise moves forward through one of the tribes of Israel, namely Judah, carrying that solution.

The Covenant of Mercy and Loving Kindness

The Book of Deuteronomy introduced another divine covenant. The Hebrew word for this covenant is *checed*, pronounced kheh'-sed. It is a covenant of mercy and loving kindness:

> *Therefore know that the Lord your God, He is God, the faithful God who keeps covenant and mercy for a thousand generations with those who love Him and keep His commandments* (Deuteronomy 7:9).

Just for loving God in return for His Love, and by keeping His commandments, we can insure His mercy and loving kindness every day for a thousand generations! Analyze that if you will! Most of us didn't know this covenant was available and in process each and every day we wake up, should we choose to love Him and receive it! It's new every morning, no matter how bad yesterday might have been.

> *Eye has not seen, nor ear heard, nor have entered into the heart of man the things which God has prepared for those who love Him* (1 Corinthians 2:9.

127

Principles of Covenant Life

(to be discussed in home groups for practical application)

1. The spirit of the law is greater than the letter of the law. You need the Holy Spirit's help to read the Scriptures in spirit and truth for its true revelation and meaning. Some of its truth is revealed between the lines.

2. The commandments were given as standards of conduct and behavior. If you break one, you are guilty of breaking them all. See James 2:10. We have all sinned and all have fallen short of the glory of God. See Romans 3:23.

3. Grace is that gift which empowers you to stay on that course with God's will, which is love.

4. If you love God and love people but your life is in confusion, don't worry. You have everything you need, even if it's out of order. Go to the Living Word, your Heart Manual from the Manufacturer Himself, and ask the Holy Spirit to bring order to your chaos.

5. Holiness and worldliness are incompatible. They are two separate kingdoms. You cannot maintain citizenship in each. You'll have to leave one behind to fully participate in the other. Each has its own king and master and you will become a slave to the one you obey.

6. As another piece to your identity and destiny, you have been pronounced and ordained a priest by God Himself. Blood Covenant relationship ratifies, endorses and authenticates this Word from God. You shall be.....if you will obey!

7. Honoring your mother and father is not based on their behavior but on who they are in that office.

8. Your spiritual heart is not only the center of your being, your spirit mind and the subconscious mind, but also is the center of your perception for seeing and hearing.

9. God is God, whether you believe it or not. You are not God, whether you believe it or not.

10. God's commandments are already written on the tablets of your heart. Ignorance is no longer an excuse for breaking them.

11. Love is a choice. It is the "tree of life" again in person. Love comes in three flavors: the Father, the Son, and the Holy Spirit. Taste and see how God it is!

12. God describes Himself as merciful, gracious, long-suffering, and abounding in goodness and truth. See Exodus 34:7. He's giving us a glimpse of ourselves, if we look into Him for our true identity, nature, and likeness.

13. There is one law that will change your heart. It's the law of love. Practice it and see how it will even help change others' hearts. It never fails!

Questions for Further Thought

1. What does it mean to you to be a "priest" ordained by God Himself?_____

_____

What affect should this identity have in your daily life?_____

_____

2. How is your relationship with your parents? Do you honor them or dishonor them?_____

_____

How does this relationship affect your relationship with your spouse and your children?

_____

What do you need to do to improve your relationship with your parents?_____

_____

Prayer

(Repeat this prayer out loud and/or add your own when led)

Come Holy Spirit, lead us into prayer!

Holy Spirit, I can see that I am helpless to keep these commandments without Your Help! Jesus, thank You for being My Savior. The law has shown me that without Your grace I will always break Your law and could not save myself. Lord, by an act of my faith and my free will, I choose to obey Your voice and keep Your covenant and commandments with Your help. You said I am a special treasure to You. I am a priest. I am holy, set apart for You, my Master, ready to do Your Will.

I'm proud to be a citizen of Your kingdom and to be in good standing. There is no other God but You. Thank You, my King, for being in residence in my body and my home. You are welcome here and I give You all authority in my heart!

Lord Jesus, I thank You for Your most precious blood! I apply it on the lintel of my forehead and mind and the *caph* of my heart. Please enter and abide in me!

Thank You for this Word today. I Love You, Lord, and I choose to love my neighbors as You have loved me, and I choose to always honor my mother and father. Thank you for my parents and for their choice of life for me.

Heavenly Father, truly You are merciful and gracious, longsuffering, and abounding in goodness and truth. Thank You for loving me and keeping Your mercy in forgiving my iniquity, transgression and sin. May I too extend this Love to all those I daily meet. I receive Your covenant of *checed*, Your mercy and loving kindness each morning that I awake. May I always be aware of Your love in my spirit mind. Thank You, Lord.

Lord, I pray for all those I love, especially ____names____, to stand in covenant one day with You. I pray that they will choose You as I have chosen You to be my Lord and Savior!

Thank You, Lord, that Your Word is not far off or a mystery to me! You have planted it deeply into my heart.

Thank You, Jesus, that while we were yet sinners, You came to earth to save us, not only from the works of the devil, but also from ourselves!

131

Thank You, Jehovah Jireh, my Provider, for always furnishing my clothes and my sandals and the food on my table. Thank You, Jesus, for being the Bread of my life! I love You! Amen.

Chapter 6

The Davidic Covenant: Love Relationship Advancing

꧁❀꧂

C are to see the fundamental ingredients of a lasting love relationship between two people? I needed to have a model, a blueprint spelled out and written down before I could understand where to start my new marriage relationship. I found the first model in the Old Testament in the person of King David.

Fourteen generations after Abraham and almost four hundred years after the death of Moses came the reign of King David, 1011-971 B.C. David, the son of Jesse, from the tribe of Judah, was a shepherd boy who became king. When God looked down upon the earth and regarded

David's heart, He chose him to be the "one" anointed to carry out His divine plan. God told King Saul, "The Lord has sought for Himself a man after His own heart" (1 Sam. 13:14). This verse in scripture was in context the reference to David, Saul's successor. God's desire was that the man who was going to carry the Seed of this covenant love relationship would be "one" after His own heart!

Have you ever considered yourself to be *one* after God's own heart? If not, would you like to continue this journey and embark in pursuit of the very heart of God? It just might take you closer to your spouse's heart. Let's revisit the scenes of the covenant Jonathan made with David and the covenant God made with David. Ask the Holy Spirit to take you there to experience these events firsthand, as if you were there that very day. Incidentally, you were there, even if you don't yet have that revelation!

In 1 Samuel 18:1-5 we read:

*Now when he (David) had finished speaking to Saul, the **soul** of Jonathan was **knit** to the **soul** of David, and Jonathan **loved him as his own soul**. Saul took him that day, and would not let him go home to his father's house anymore. Then Jonathan and David made a covenant, because he loved him as his own soul. And Jonathan took off his **robe** that was on him and gave it to David, with his **armor**, even to his **sword** and his **bow** and his **belt**. So David went out wherever Saul sent him, and behaved **wisely**. And Saul set him over the men of war, and he was accepted in the sight of all the people and also in the sight of Saul's servants (1 Samuel 18:1-5 emphasis added).*

This scripture passage is loaded with God's principles of relationship. We must put each verse under the microscope now to see God's deeper covenant ingredients.

Verse One

First, we see in verse one that when one person makes a choice from his heart to love another, there releases into the spirit realm a seed of desire for a heart tie or bond in one's heart. The Hebrew word for soul is "*nephesh*." It translates as one's entire being: spirit, soul and body. When this intimation is received by the other person, an actual knitting together of hearts takes place. You can't see it in the natural, but it is a spiritual reality. The conception having taken place results in the two individuals being knitted together, becoming one unit that is inseparable, united in identity.

I would like to quote my wife, Jill, regarding the practical meaning of that word inseparable. She said:

When I met Robert, and by the way I wasn't looking for anyone, I realized something was happening to me while we were talking. I felt like I was being drawn by his every word and I felt his words were affecting my heart. Our conversation continued for about three hours. We talked about life and about everything that was important to me. I never before had met a man who could communicate this well. I was able to express myself from my heart and then he would reply with understanding. My experience with him was really comfortable.

After that first encounter I didn't hear from him for quite some time. But I couldn't stop thinking about that conversation and his words. I tried to shake him off but couldn't find the shut-off button. I had this feeling for him that I couldn't explain. How can I feel this way after just meeting him once? I desired him. I wanted to know more about him. I didn't realize it at the time but there had been a seed planted in my heart. At that moment I knew my heart was knitted to him. And even though I had only seen him once, I felt I had known him all my life. To me it was love at first sight and that proved to be true.

This wasn't a miracle. This was a decision made freely from one's heart. Here we simply see the sowing and reaping process. Loving words can eventually give birth to relationship. This process was designed by the very nature of God's Own Heart for the benefit of His children. This is a description of the heart bond between God and His people, spirit, soul and body! With us! With you! With me! The "Seed" sent out was Jesus! We simply have to receive Him totally in response!

> *Who shall separate us from the love of Christ?...For I am persuaded that neither death nor life, nor angels nor* **principalities** *nor* **powers***, nor things present nor things to come, nor height nor depth, nor any other created thing, shall be able to separate us from the love of God which is in Christ Jesus our Lord* (Romans 8:35a, 39 emphasis added).

We are bonded to God, knitted to God, Soul to soul, Heart to heart, given His identity, with "Who He is," through Him, with Him, in Him, together abiding in His Love! Can you fathom that? It is possible! You'll have to read chapter 7 to see how. There is a scheme, however, and a struggle to break this bond with God and with each other that has been in effect since the first episode with the serpent and man back in Eden. Ephesians 6:10-12 gives further reference to the villain of this love story and his counterfeit plan that is managed through *principalities*, *powers*, rulers of the darkness of this age, against spiritual hosts of wickedness in the heavenly places as highlighted above.

Verse Two

Verse two showed that King Saul took David that day and would not let him go home to his father's house anymore. Do you get it? Once the King and His Son take you in, you become joint heir to their kingdom. You have become an adopted child through covenant with the King Himself through His Son. Now you're getting it! Everything the King has, including all rights of kingdom citizenship, become yours because the King chose you! You don't have to accept. If you should, however, you actually will then belong to the King and are no longer under the authority of your earthly parents. It is then proper for you to "leave to cleave." (Note: even when we are under the authority of our parents, all authority comes from God. Proper leaving and blessing of the parents are paramount in cleaving to the King and His authority. We never belong

We are bonded to God, knitted to God, Soul to soul, Heart to heart, given His identity, with "Who He is", through Him, with Him, in Him, together abiding in His Love!

137

to our parents. They are simply the King's *agents* to impart His identity and blessings.)

Verses Three and Four

In verse three the covenant was made and in verse four another significant exchange took place. Jonathan, the covenant initiator, took off the *robe* (the kingly robe which is a direct reference to the King's Son, Jesus, the Blood Covenant Initiator, whose robe was taken off at Calvary, but now He gives it to us to wear—His royal robe of righteousness, covering and protection) that was on him and gave it to David, his covenant partner. He then proceeded to give David his *armor*, even his *sword*, and his *bow* and *belt*. (See also Eph. 6:13-17.)

You have become an adopted child through covenant with the King Himself through His Son…Everything the King has, including all rights of kingdom citizenship, become yours because the King chose you!

We now have all the armor of Jesus, including His Word—a two-edged sword. The King freely relinquished these prize *possessions* and *weapons* with their symbolic royalty *rights*! Your sword, bow, and weapon belt were even more valuable considering the backdrop of warfare, which was rampant, with self-defense being necessary for your very survival. Obviously, those possessions of Jonathan, the king's son, were more elegant than David's.

138

The covenant tradition of that day was that each person made an exchange of things of value. Thus David, also, had to make a comparable exchange. All David had of value to exchange, as a poor shepherd boy, was his heart. He and Jonathan took an oath, similar to the Native Americans as blood brothers, never to pick up or use their weapons against each other, even in self-defense.

Verse Five

Finally, in verse five David went out in Saul's name and behaved wisely. David had "power of attorney," so to speak, and carried the King's *name* representatively, so that wherever he went he conducted himself accordingly. He had been given all the authority in the King's name and the power that goes with it. My! What a powerful exchange! What a great deal for David! Especially considering his position in warfare! (See a further illustration of this in the *Covenant* section that follows.)

Let's bring the focus a little closer to home now for the practical application to our relationships with each other. We'll use marriage as an example. Each person should:

1. Have God *help* in choosing your covenant marriage partner;

2. Freely choose to love the other with *all* your heart;

3. Make a marriage covenant so a righteous *bonding* will occur;

4. Take on a *new identity* as two souls knit together;

5. Willingly *leave* your father's house to *cleave* to each other;

139

6. Begin to love each other as your own three-part being, spirit, soul and body, second only to God.

7. (The covenant initiator) Exchange his vows and promise to give her, "*All* he *has* and *all* that he *is*." He will give her his *name* (power of attorney), his *rights* and *authority*, all of his *possessions*, his *protection*, and will not use his *weapons* against her. He will present her to be accepted in the sight of all people as his wife (*honor* her worth);

Are we willing in humility and submission to relinquish our possessions, rights and weapons for this highest standard of relationship?

8. (The covenant partner) Exchange her vows and promise to give him, "*All* she *has* and *all* that *she* is." She will take his *name* wherever she goes and *behave wisely*! She will *submit* to the *authority* that her husband is under (the authority of Jesus Christ) and is willing to give up all of her *possessions* and *rights* and will not use any *weapon* against him. She will present him to be accepted in the sight of all the people as her husband (*honor* his worth);

9. Vow that this agreement is *forever*, 'til death. (See 1 Sam. 20:42.)

Where should we stand on these points? There are many more of course. Are we willing in humility and submission to relinquish our possessions, rights and weapons for this highest standard of relationship? David and Jonathan were! God is! (Don't miss the section on *Rights, Weapons, and Possessions.*)

Did you notice who the covenant initiator was? It was Jonathan! Remember, in a "Love Covenant," Jonathan would be in a position of strength and authority and could thereby offer more to his covenant partner in blessings in exchange as a result. In other words, it was done decently and in the proper order! Here in the scenario that follows is an example of why some relationships, without these considerations, are subject to failure:

Once upon a time, there was a guy named Bill,

Who fell in love with a gal named Lil!

They met at a dance. It was love at first glance as they started a romance,

However, they failed to ask God, "Was this Your will?"

It was not yet the right time, for Bill had not a dime,

But Lil pursued him, she said, for the thrill!

Not planning to marry, now Bill's baby she'd carry,

And wondered just what her parents would think!

Next came baby Sue; neither knew what to do,

Their relationship now began to sink!

When she got no support, they proceeded to court,

Since their love had diminished, the romance was finished!

Bill just couldn't be bothered, so Sue wasn't fathered,

But Lil's heart has to deal with it still!

How many people do you know who fall into this seemingly fictitious scenario? Most of the people in the "baby boomer" generation and their descendants are living this! It's out of order! Ignorance can destroy the heart. If only God's will would have been sought first! If only the covenant initiator would have taken his responsibility, while under the King's authority, (or with parents' approval), to be in a position of strength to exercise self-discipline, maturity and timing! If only the woman had desired to be in her Father's Will, with her parents' blessing, with the patience to wait for the man to be prepared and molded as the King so desires! Who's going to mend all these broken hearts? How long will all parties, especially the innocent ones, the babies, have to pay the consequences for these foolish choices? As the Israelites back then, we too haven't grasped God's divine ways.

It is very important to note that even after Jonathan died, King David honored their covenant.

> *Now David said, "Is there **anyone** left of the **house** of Saul, that I may show him kindness for Jonathan's sake?"...Now when Mephibosheth the son of Jonathan, the son of Saul, had come to David, he fell on his face and prostrated himself. Then David said, "Mephibosheth?" And he answered, "Here is your servant!" So David said to him, "Do not fear, for I will surely show you kindness for Jonathan your father's sake, and will **restore** to you **all the land** of Saul your grandfather; and you shall eat **bread** at **my table continually**"* (1 Sam. 9:1, 6-7 emphasis added).

Just think! Where would you be if your grandfather and father had just died? You were *lame in both feet* (the meaning of Mephibosheth's name). The spirit of death and abandonment had overwhelmed you and fear was tormenting you. Now, who are you, where do you belong, and where will you go? To whom do you turn for help? This is what Mephibosheth faced. Just what does happen to all those who are left behind by death, that are orphaned or victims of divorce? Are they disinherited, disconnected and written off by former family members? What becomes of all those relatives when death or divorce occurs? Some people try to erase them from the records and sweep them under the carpet to hide them from memory. Fortunately for us and for Mephibosheth, these are not God's ways nor David's, the man after God's own heart!

As we saw earlier, the power of blood covenant continues beyond death. It handles all survivors with love and compassion and, rather than abandonment, makes them a joint heir and reinstates them in one's household with a place of honor and welcomes them to the dinner table. Mephibosheth, as a rightful heir, did not demand those privileges, but humbly lay prostrate before the king in gratitude. We can learn from him. David's unconditional love transcended the death of Jonathan, his covenant partner. Please do not reject but embrace and espouse the victims of death and divorce. Make room in your heart for them to sit at your table. Include them! Love them! Covenant has commitment to the next generation of children and insures provision, protection, and love to be available and in place even when a partner dies.

Up to this time, this was the most well known covenant between two people. However, we need to proceed to the Davidic covenant that God made with King David.

> *But it happened that night that the **word** of the Lord came to Nathan, saying, "Go and tell My servant David, 'Thus says the Lord: "Would you build a **house** for Me to dwell in? For I have not dwelt in a house since the time that I brought the children of Israel up from Egypt, even to this day, but have moved about in a tent and in a tabernacle. Wherever I have moved about with all the children of Israel, have I ever spoken a word to anyone from the tribes of Israel, whom I commanded to shepherd My people Israel, saying, 'Why have you not built Me a house of cedar?'"" Now therefore, thus shall you say to my servant David, 'Thus says the Lord of hosts: "I took you from the sheepfold, from following the sheep, to be ruler over My people, over Israel. "And I have been with you wherever you have gone, and have **cut off all your enemies** from before you, and have made you a great name, like the name of the great men who are on the earth. Moreover I will appoint a place for My people Israel, and will plant them, that they may **dwell** in a **place** of their own and **move no more**; nor shall the sons of wickedness oppress them anymore, as previously, since the time that I have commanded judges over My people Israel, and have caused you to rest from **all** your enemies. Also the Lord tells you that He will make you a **house**. When your days are fulfilled and you rest with your fathers, I will set up your **seed** after you, who will*

come from your body, and I will establish his king-
dom. "He (Solomon) shall build a house for My name,
*and I will establish the **throne** of his kingdom **for-***
***ever**. "I will be his **Father**, and He shall be My **son**.*
If he commits iniquity, I will chasten him with the rod
of men and with the blows of the sons of men. But
*My **mercy** (checed) shall not depart from him, as I*
took it from Saul, whom I removed from before you.
And your house and your kingdom shall be estab-
lished forever before you. Your throne shall be estab-
*lished **forever**.'""" According to all these words and*
according to all this vision, so Nathan spoke to David
(2 Samuel 7:4-17 emphasis added).

David responded gratefully to the Lord's words and received them all. (See 2 Sam. 7:18-19.) Notice all the highlighted words in the above verses. The covenant that God made promised by His Word to cut off *all* our enemies (protection); to dwell in a place of their own and to move no more (a blessed land as an inheritance; think of all the trouble God's children have experienced in foreign lands for not obeying *that* Word! Disastrous! Catastrophic!); your family, or house (household) and seed (the seed containing the promise) will be blessed and continue forever; and your throne (kinship in the kingdom with the King Himself) will be established forever and ever!

The end of the first act, or Old Testament (Covenant) draws to a close. The stage has been set. The themes of promise, faithfulness to one's word, covenant relationship and love have been established and have endured. And now, before the curtain falls on Act One, Jeremiah the prophet, whose ministry stretched from about 627 to 580

B.C., would like to make the following announcements inspired by the Holy Spirit:

"Behold, the days are coming," says the Lord, "that I will raise to David a branch of righteousness; a King shall reign and prosper, and execute judgment and righteousness in the earth. In His days Judah will be saved, and Israel will dwell safely; Now this is His name by which He will be called: The Lord Our Righteousness (Jeremiah 23:5-6).

*"Behold, the days are coming, says the Lord, when I will make a **new covenant** with the house of Israel and with the house of Judah—not according to the covenant that I made with their fathers in the day that I took them by the hand to lead them out of the land Egypt, My covenant which they broke, though I was a **husband** to them, says the Lord. But this is the **covenant** that I will make with the house of Israel after those days, says the Lord: I will put My **Law** in their **minds**, and **write** it on their **hearts**; and **I will be their God**, and **they shall be My people**. "No more shall every man teach his neighbor, and every man his brother, saying, 'Know the Lord,' for **they shall all know Me**, from the least of them to the greatest of them, says the Lord. For **I will forgive their iniquity**, and **their sin I will remember no more**"* (Jeremiah 31:31-34 emphasis added).

The New Covenant is on the way. It will be a better covenant that the preceding ones.

146

It will be one written on our hearts. It will replace all unrighteousness, iniquity and sin with righteousness. It is "good news" to the troubled heart!

Covenant

Over one hundred years ago, Stanley, while searching for Doctor Livingston in Africa, wrote about blood covenant in his memoirs. The story briefly goes something like this: It seemed that every time Stanley would try to sell his goods throughout Africa, hostile tribes would show up and steal them. It was a constant struggle, accompanied with the obvious problems of the African jungle and terrain, to maintain their very survival. When their supplies were stolen, rather than lose their lives to possibly cannibalistic warring tribes, they chose not to fight back.

Seeking a solution to this dilemma, Stanley appealed to his African guide. His guide suggested that he should make a blood covenant with one of the chiefs of a warrior tribe for protection. Having no knowledge of the practice of making a blood covenant, he further inquired of the guide, "Just what is this blood covenant?" The guide proceeded to describe it in graphic detail. He said that the two parties would first cut their wrists, spilling their blood into a cup or such and thereby commingling the blood of each person. They would then even drink the blood to seal their relationship. This, of course, did not appeal to Stanley, and he discarded that endeavor.

Later, however, after repeated thefts and frustration, he succumbed. He asked the guide to find a powerful chief to covenant with. When he was brought to the chief and his

147

tribe, he asked the guide if there was anything else he should know. The guide proceeded to inform Stanley that the chief would require something of value exchanged as a part of the ritual. Stanley thought, why not! Anything he had was going to be stolen sooner or later anyway!

He did have one great concern, however. See, Stanley had stomach ulcers and had to bring a goat with him on his expeditions. He desperately needed goat milk to soothe his ulcers and stress. Surely the chief would not ask for that goat! Wouldn't you know it, his worst fear came true. The chief wanted the goat! "Great," he thought, "now I am not going to be eaten alive but will die from ulcers!"

What would Stanley do now? The chief took the goat and gave Stanley an eight-foot-long spear wrapped with copper wire that was almost too heavy to lift. Stanley concluded that not only was he going to die, but if he had to use this huge heavy spear against someone, it would be a worse death. Anyway, the covenant having been cut, he went on his way.

Some time later he confronted another tribe and was about to be robbed again, but when the tribe saw the spear and its markings, they immediately recognized its origin. They bowed down to the authority of the chief represented by his spear. We find out that the spear of a chief not only represents his *authority*, but his *power*. It was, to a chief, his most *valuable* possession! Now the spear in and of itself did not have the power! The power was only as great as the *chief* who *shed* his *blood*! You see, the blood symbolized the very life of the chief. The chief's spear was the sign of his covenant with Stanley. All the tribes honored this covenant and Stanley received free passage and favor wherever he traveled from that time forward.

In some regions in Africa, blood covenants still are made. To break one of these covenants, the penalty remains severe: death. An offended covenant partner and his family have the right to hunt down a covenant-breaker and kill him on the spot, and in some cases kill his children and descendants for several generations. Even a mother will turn in her own son who has broken covenant, so she would not be killed. They take their word and oath seriously! Life or death hang in the balance.

Cannibalism has been practiced by some tribes found in remote territories of Africa. The origin of this practice was the belief that if they ate a person or his blood they would receive that person's good qualities as their own. They believed there was a transfer somehow by eating of a man's flesh or some organ, such as the heart. The greater the character was of the man, the more desirable was the exchange of those attributes. Maybe this is where we got the saying, "You are what you eat!" They believed that if you ate the physical properties of the person, such as his brain, that the spiritual transfer would take effect in their brain! That's a tough concept to chew on! In other words, it was not a compliment to be asked for dinner, for you might be the main course!

Rights, Weapons and Possessions

This section serves as a guide or checklist of things that must be considered for harmony in a love relationship. Some people find this section very difficult to accomplish. There is always a cost and a price to pay for quality. See if you would be willing to unselfishly begin this menu for right relationship. Here are examples of rights, weapons and possessions that you must be willing to *relinquish* in a *Covenant Marriage*:

Relinquish the right to:

- Control my own time
- Sleep when I want to
- Control my money separately
- Maintain my reputation

Relinquish the right to withhold the following:

- Physical affection
- Sexual intimacy and pleasure
- Open communication and feelings
- Honesty
- Recreational companionship
- Money or bank accounts
- Domestic peace and quiet
- Adequate family time
- Admiration and esteem
- Access to any prized possession

Weapons you have used to protect yourself or attack your spouse to be laid down:

- Isolation
- Self pity
- Criticism
- Crying

- Dishonor

- Hardness of heart

- Anger

- Shame

- Unforgiveness

- Manipulation, Control

- Bitterness

- Bribes

- Threats

- The Tongue

Possessions you need to relinquish and lay down when out of order:

- Your will

- Your time

- Your children

- Your job as #1 priority

- Your vehicle

- Your ministry

- Your chair

- The T.V. remote control

- Your money

- Your relatives, friends

Note: Some of these listed can be used as all three: right, weapon, and possession!

Principles of Covenant Life

(to be discussed in home groups for practical application)

1. God' plan is bonding! The enemy's scheme is bondage! You are subject to one or the other in relationships. Love creates and nourishes bonding. Fear creates and nourishes bondage. Perfect love casts out fear. The blood of Jesus breaks the curse of the spirit of fear and bondage. Jesus is perfect love.

2. Both bonding and bondage have holding power. They are as strong as the master you've chosen to obey. You become a slave to the master you believe in. Your beliefs are rooted in your heart. Choose the right "Master."

3. Nothing can separate God's love from you! He's already made that decision.

4. You, however, can separate yourself from His love by turning your back on Him and refusing to receive it as your decision and choosing darkness instead! That's called the spirit of stupid!

5. Covenant governs your three-part being: spirit, soul and body. It has been written indelibly on your heart by the Holy Spirit. Boot up your mind and see how God put His Laws there. Ignorance of God's Laws is no longer an acceptable excuse.

6. In a covenant marriage relationship, since God is included in the triangle, whenever you pick up a weapon against your spouse, be aware that you are picking it up against God first! Knowing this is how covenant relationship works makes it easier for you to lay down weapons, rights and possessions in obe-

dience to God first! Besides, God and your spouse have you outnumbered!

7. Covenant is a spiritual hedge of protection put in place by God. His Word says He will cut off all your enemies! They can't get through the hedge or the walls of the hedge. It's like having the walls of His kingdom around you and your family. There's no guarantee if you choose to go outside these walls. It keeps the enemy out and you in.

8. Not only is your covenant eternal and everlasting, but also the new love you will experience will never fade or diminish within its confines.

9. The cup of your covenant love spills over upon your children, out to your extended family, upon your friends, and upon everyone you influence. It continues to spill out even after death and never quits working. This is the cup of Life filled for us with the blood of Jesus!

Questions for Further Thought

1. Which word best characterizes your marriage: bonding or bondage? _____ Since love creates and nourishes bonding, what specific things will you do to express love to your spouse on a consistent basis? _____

   _____

2. What "weapons" do you use to control or manipulate your spouse?_____
   Are you willing to lay them down even if your spouse

is not yet ready to do the same?_____

_____

Prayer

Please put together a list of your rights, weapons and possessions *before* praying this Prayer.

(Repeat this prayer out loud and/or add your own when led)

Holy Spirit, take us to our Father's Heart!

Heavenly Father, it is I, one after Your own heart! I want to feel Your love at each beat of Your heart. I am bonded to You so closely that my heart is knitted to Yours. Thank You for taking me in to Your house and Kingdom. I will worship You at Your throne forever as My King. You are my Father and I am Your son. Thank You for settling that in my heart as my true identity. I never wish to leave anymore.

Thank You, Lord, for this revelation from the Davidic covenant and the covenant between Jonathan and David. Lord, I choose to behave wisely wherever You send me in Your name.

Father, I understand that whenever I pick up a weapon against my brother, it is You that I use it against first. Holy Spirit, help me not to pick up any weapons against my brothers and sisters. Let my weapons be mighty in God to fight against strongholds of the flesh and my adversary's works.

I freely choose, with Your help and as You lead me, to lay down the following weapons that I either have used against my brothers and sisters or my spouse or picked up to defend myself.......(names)........

I lay down the following possessions at Your feet......(names)........ I further relinquish the following rights that You have brought to my conviction......(names).........

I acknowledge using these weapons, holding on to these possessions, and not relinquishing these rights, as sin. I ask Your forgiveness, Lord. I receive Your blood, Jesus, to cover these sins. Holy Spirit, please make me aware of what I have laid down, so that I will not pick them up again. Do not let these come between my heart and Yours again. Jesus, You are my defense, and I choose not to defend myself or to offend others.

(If your spouse is available, and if you are
led by the Holy Spirit, say:)

I also ask your forgiveness,.......(spouse)........, for using these weapons.....(names)......against you and defending myself. I have held on to these possessions, ...(names)...., and I choose to let them go. I freely relinquish these rights.......(names)........as they no longer are rights to me. I confess all of these as sin. I ask your forgiveness. I love you and pray they will never come between our hearts as wedges any longer.

Thank You, Lord, for Your truth that has set me free! Amen.

Chapter 7

The New Covenant: Jesus Christ, Our Righteousness

≈≈⊱⊰≈≈

What does a man do when he really loves a woman and knows that she also loves him, yet together they just can't seem to keep the relationship going peacefully without every other day screaming and fighting? I didn't know. I looked for any solution or equation to bring my marriage to some semblance of stability. It was a daily roller coaster ride and the hills were getting steeper and the valleys lower and the cars were about to derail. There had to be a way that worked better than the cyclical pattern that had failed me in the past! Where could I go and what could I do to stop this bittersweet melodrama?

157

So many times I've asked myself, "Is that all there is?" Sounds like the old Peggy Lee tune, doesn't it? Her conclusion was, "Then let's break out the booze and have a ball, if that's all there is!" Isn't that what most of us do? Help! God help me! If only we had gone to Him first instead of last!

Just when it didn't seem like the love affair between God and mankind was ever going to be reconciled and restored to its original state, the Covenant Initiator, the Lord God Jehovah, Himself, arrived on the earth scene! The *Seed* He had promised to Adam, to Noah, to Abraham, to Moses, to David and to their descendants was to become manifest and be born to Joseph and Mary of the house of David. Finally, twenty eight generations after David, the event took place in God's own way and fashion. Since man couldn't save himself from himself, the Manufacturer Himself had to come down, become flesh, and repair him spirit, soul and body.

Immanuel

Almost 700 years before Christ was born, Scripture told us of His coming:" Therefore the Lord Himself will give you a sign: Behold, the virgin shall conceive and bear a Son, and shall call His name Immanuel" (Is. 7:14), which means "God with us." What a climax! What a promise! What a deal! "God with us"! Not figuratively or invisibly but Jehovah, the God of the Blood Covenant in Person, with arms and legs!

There is a Greek word, *diatithemai* that describes this phenomenon. *Dia* means "covenant" and *tithemai*, "to place between two" or "cut." Jesus was that Covenant cut and placed between God and man. He was the Bridge between God and man, the Bridge over troubled waters, so to speak. He is the Mediator of a New Covenant, the weaving that knit man's spirit back to God's Spirit.

The Incarnation

Jesus is the New Covenant and the new beginning for man! He's called the second Adam, the new genesis of mankind. Jesus perfectly reestablished man's original identity, destiny, purpose and potential. Mary provided Jesus with His physical human genetics and by the power of the Holy Spirit the Seed received its divine spiritual genetics and bloodline as Christ, the Anointed One. Thus, Jesus Christ! Jesus, man! Christ, God! Yet One! God-man! The *Incarnation*! What a reality! It took 4000 years to prepare for the manifestation of that reality that **was** *in the beginning*! "In the beginning was the *Word*, and the *Word* was *with* God, and the *Word was God*...And the *Word* became *flesh* and *dwelt among us*, and we beheld His *glory*, the *glory* as of the *only begotten* of the *Father*, full of grace and truth" (Jn. 1:1, 14 emphasis added). Finally, the *glory* that was lost in *Eden* is now going to be *restored* by the *presence of Jesus* among us!

He is the Mediator of a New Covenant, the weaving that knit man's spirit back to God's Spirit.

When nothing was going right, it was because my heart wasn't right. Every problem is associated with a heart problem. I'm not referring to your physical ticker but your

159

spirit heart. The issues of life originate from what you believe in your heart. The whole time I was feeling terrible, disconnected, and like a wanderer on planet Earth, I was looking for the answers to my heart's dilemma on the out-side. What I was lacking and what I needed was something on the inside. I needed to eat of the "Tree of Life" so I could begin living my life from the inside out. I needed to ask the author of my life to cross over the threshold of my heart and make His home there to be Lord of my life. I needed to partake of the New Covenant.

Our New Covenant

Let's break this awesome reality down into smaller pieces to consume! Covenant is the outworking of the very nature of God! The Holy Trinity itself is a covenant rela-tionship! The Father, Son and Holy Spirit made a covenant agreement to make man in Their own "image and like-ness." That's us! The Father said, "I will if You will." The Son said, "I will if You will." The Holy Spirit said, "I will if You will." That's His will! God swore by Himself in the presence of Jesus the High Priest.

We have seen what a covenant is: a holy, sacred, irrevo-cable, unbreakable agreement between two or more parties. Can you now see that its identity and source are the nature and likeness of God Himself? We have discussed several kinds of covenants: a covenant of hospitality, a threshold covenant, a blood covenant, a love covenant, a covenant of mercy and loving-kindness. Again, they all flow from the character and essence of God. Some of the covenant compo-nents were: the presence of a witness or high priest (*Elohim*), a spoken word (*Word*), oath or vow, the altar of sacrifice or offering (*Calvary*), the sacrificial cutting of an animal in two (*the Lamb*), the ratification by blood of the agreement (*Jesus' shed blood* on the cross), the exchange of gifts (*life for death*), the promise or document being sealed (*Pentecost*), the meal of sharing bread and wine (*the Lord's Supper*), a covenant sign (*a reborn, resurrected Spirit*)! Such a wondrous beautiful plan! What an inheritance!

We have seen who makes a covenant and why: those who need protection, the weak tribe with the strong tribe (Now we are under the authority of *Jesus*, the *Warrior King*, the **Lion** from the *tribe of Judah*); those who need a stronger party in a business relationship (*Jehovah Jireh, the Provider Himself*); and those who for the sheer sake of love desire to covenant with a weaker vessel to pour out blessings (*Love in Person now blesses us*). Can you receive that into your spirit for your true identity?

The attitude of all covenant partners in the following statements are the sentiments of God Himself: *"All that I have and all that I am are yours." "I will, if you will." "If you need it, you come and ask for it; My house is open to you at all hours." "Knock, anytime and I'll give you bread." I'm making a commitment to you and am willing to die for that commitment." "My very Life is at stake here and I would rather die than break this covenant."* Can you hear the heart of the King? Is this your heart's attitude?

There were seven (7) covenants in the Old Testament, a divine number of completion. Jesus was the eighth covenant in the New Testament, the divine number for the new beginning! He both fulfilled and was the completion of the other seven. Remember, not one Word of His will pass

161

away! Hebrews 1:3 in the *Amplified Bible* says that Jesus Christ is the "sole expression of the glory of God—the Light-being, the out-raying of the divine—and he is the perfect imprint and very image of God's nature..."And to think, some still believe He is not God!

The Last Supper, The Covenant Meal

These were the words spoken by Jesus at the Last Supper scene as He shared His final covenant meal with His disciples during the feast of the Passover:

> *And as they were eating, Jesus took **bread**, blessed and broke it, and gave it to the disciples and said, "Take, **eat**; this is **My body**"* (Mt. 26:26).

(In Luke 22:19 Jesus says, "This is My body which is *given* for you.)

> *Then He took the **cup**, and gave thanks, and gave it to them, saying, "Drink from it, all of you. "For this is **My blood** of the **new covenant**, which is **shed** for many for the remission of sins* (Mt. 26:27-28).

(In Luke 22:20 Jesus says, "This cup is the new covenant in My blood, which is shed for you.")

He was the Lamb, whose body was to be broken and sacrificed at the altar of Calvary. So also the **b**lood was His, for it is blood of the New Covenant, Jesus Himself! These words make little sense in the natural realm, but in the spiritual realm it made more sense to the apostles, who in this context were more than familiar with the concept of Blood Covenant. The moment these words were spoken, chills must have rushed through their bodies even with their still limited understanding.

The Garden of Gethsemane

After the supper they sang a hymn and then went out into the Mount of Olives to a place called Gethsemane. Isn't it ironic that this moment spent by Jesus in prayer in *this* garden before His death was the result of man's disobedience in *another* garden in Eden? From the first garden He, who was and is the "tree of life," was the One sent from this garden to be nailed upon another tree, a tree of death, like the tree "of the knowledge of good and evil"! Imagine the torment and bitter cup Jesus had to drink here for man's choice! Worse yet, He was to become a substitute for sin! A holy God, who never knew sin, to be made sin for our sake! Now comes the further horror of being separated from His Father for the first time. His heart was so much in travail that He sweated blood. However, Jesus endured it all in obedience and carried out His Father's will.

About two years after my second divorce, I was sitting alone in the living room of my house on one of the most desolate days of my life. All of a sudden the ringing of the phone broke the solitude. It was Jill. She could always sense my emotional condition with discerning accuracy. She suggested I take two weeks off from my friends and from hanging out at night in the bar scene. Further, she encouraged me to pick up my Bible and read the entire gospel of John. "When you finish reading John, call me," she concluded.

I spent the next two weeks alone talking to God and reading His Word. It was my Gethsemane. In the beginning

I felt I was somewhere way out there in space, totally alone, drifting nowhere, going though a whole spectrum of familiar emotions. It was very uncomfortable at first to be left exclusively with my thoughts. However, there was a peace that came with reading that Gospel. Day after day I actually started to feel that I was not alone. Something on the inside was about to die and be crucified. My thoughts, because I finally took time to deal with them, at moments overwhelmed me.

When I finished the last chapter and the last sentence of John, something immediately happened to me. A warmth came over me, a kind of euphoric feeling of peace and joy that made me flash back to the time God spoke to me that night in Vietnam. It was happening all over again! A God touch! I experienced a death to my oppression and a revival in my heart. I called Jill at once and told her what had taken place. It was the beginning of a new communication towards our marriage reconciliation, but it was going to take a long before the process was completed.

The Betrayal, Arrest, and Denial of Jesus

Isn't it interesting in times of distress to see which people you consider to be friends actually are there when you need help ever so desperately? They thin out real quickly when you covet their rescue. There was one of Jesus' own apostles, whom He had chosen to love and die for that night, who would reject His love and betray Him. Judas Iscariot not only dipped in the dish with Jesus during the covenant meal but also betrayed the Lord God Almighty with a kiss. The spirit of greed (mammon) entered him and he sold His God for thirty pieces of silver. When Judas and the soldiers came to arrest Him, Jesus said, "I am He" (John 18:6), and they all fell to the ground, overwhelmed by the power of the Spirit of God! Later, even Peter would deny Jesus three times. Imagine the hurt Jesus experienced from His best friends!

When I made this covenant commitment to Jesus and to Jill, my friends thought I was crazy. My softball cronies made the remark, "Scheck left the team and is now playing for the Saints." There is a cost when you decide to leave your play world behind and get serious about life and the people in it. There comes a time to put the ball glove and cleats away and grow up. All the trophies I received over the years went into the trash because they were a sore reminder of my selfishness as a priority over family. The problem wasn't my friends but the world they represented when I chose to be with them instead of my wife. Losing my friends hurt at first but I realized then that we no longer had much in common. Nevertheless, the words they spoke behind my back were nothing compared to what Jesus experienced.

The Crucifixion: The Cutting of the Blood Covenant

The crucifixion of Jesus is the most disgraceful subject our spirit and soul have to comprehend. I have difficulty even writing about it. It was at the same time both the greatest tragedy and the greatest victory. It was the most tragic demonstration in history of the wickedness in the heart of the human race.

Jesus Christ, Jehovah Jehoshua Mashiach, the Unrecognized Love Covenant Initiator with Israel, whom they knew as a young boy and saw being circumcised into their own Covenant, yet they chose to kill Him! He had walked among them, His own people, to save them from death! Yet He was despised, rejected, unjustly accused, spat upon, beaten, stripped, ridiculed, mocked, scourged, and nailed to the cross! He was an innocent man, without sin, yet was given the most humiliating and excruciating punishment ever devised by man: death on a cross, naked and exposed for all to see! This was the most shameful day in the annals of man! This was the tree mankind should have died upon for his rebellion. Instead, Jesus freely laid down His life for us!

Despite all of this agony and pain, the true character and heart of Jesus prevailed as He said, "Father, forgive them, for they do not know what they do." (Lk. 23:34). This model of forgiveness can only come from Agape Love Himself! Forgiveness should become automatic for one who calls himself a Christian. It's not an option for a disciple.

Now from the sixth hour until the ninth hour there was darkness all over the land. And about the ninth hour Jesus cried out with a loud voice, saying, "Eli. Eli. Lama sabachthani?" that is, "My God, My God, why have You forsaken Me?" (Mt. 27:45-46).

This was the first time the Son of God was ever separated from His Father. It was necessary in order for Him to become the *Substitute* for *sin* and for *us*, His covenant partners. Envision, if you can, the horror and torment of that spirit of abandonment when sin separated God from

God! The ultimate death for each person! How much Love this must have taken! Immeasurable! Boundless!

> *So when Jesus had received the sour wine, He said, "It is finished!" And bowing His head, He gave up His spirit.* (Jn. 19:30).

His mission was accomplished! The Blood Covenant was perfectly cut and executed! The "Lamb" that was slain before the foundations of the world completed His Love Promise in obedience to His own Word! Our Savior! Our Redeemer! Our Deliverer! Our Master! Our Hero! Our King! There aren't enough superlatives in all the languages of the world combined to express our gratitude for this consummated ransom of our debt! Thank You Jesus, for giving us **LIFE**!

[Separation from His Father] was necessary in order for [Jesus] to become the Substitute for sin and for us, His covenant partners.

Pentecost, the Promise Fulfilled

Into the upper room, where the apostles, the women, Mary, the mother of Jesus and His brothers had gathered with one accord, "suddenly there came a sound from heaven, as of a rushing mighty wind....and they were all filled with the Holy Spirit" (Acts 2:2-4). They were reborn by the "power" of the Holy Spirit just as Jesus had promised. This sealed the Blood Covenant. Their spirits were reunited with God. It was a family reunion. Now, in power, they will walk in the Spirit. A reborn spirit was to be the *sign* of the New Covenant.

167

How do I walk in covenant?

Many are called but few are chosen. Covenant is available to everyone, but a death is required for its full benefit.

We must relate to God based on what He said and what He did! [We] relate to God through covenant!

It's not going to be easy, just worth it. It'll take resolve and discipline and will come at a cost. There will still be arguing at times but you have something always to refer to as your standard of covenant behavior. If you say, "I don't know if I can give it up; I'm having a battle with this," you do not have covenant commitment. Give it up! Let it go! Surrender! Submit! Yield! Put the other person ahead of you. You're not doing God a favor by getting rid of your manure. Do yourself a favor. There is great revelation in seeing your flesh as God sees it. Filthy stinking rags! Take them off humbly in exchange for His kingly robe of righteousness!

In a love covenant neither party has to be a beggar. You are valuable. It's already yours. Your attitude should not be to go to Calvary just for fire insurance to miss hell. You should not go only for blessings or all the fringe benefits. You should go for the sheer sake of returning all the love you have for Him who died for your life. He has made a love deposit in your name in heaven's bank. You have free checking and are able to sign His name on the checks!

Covenant parties mutually agree that neither party will infringe upon, presume, or steal from the other. Let your yes be yes and your no be no. Let your word be as is His Word. We must relate to God based on what He *said* and

168

what He *did*! I repeat, I relate to God on what He *says*, what He *did*, and *who He is*! Relationship comes not by *works*—what you *do*—or by what you *deserve*. I repeat: not my works, what I have *done*, am *doing*, or *failed to do*! I relate to God through covenant!

God wants union of being again with us in Jesus. He wants His family back—reborn. We pray that you'll never be the same after this revelation of Blood Covenant. We pray that Holy Communion will have the deepest of meanings to you from this day forward as you sup with Him at the banquet table of mercy! Every time the bread is broken and the wine is taken, we pray that your eyes will be opened to see Jesus! We pray that by taking this journey you have come to know Him intimately! Where do we go from here? Let's go to the final chapter of the Bible for our ultimate destination! *There's still a wedding coming!*

Covenant—Did you Know?

Did you know that there is in man an innate knowledge—something that is resident within all peoples of the earth—that there is a Supreme Being and that there has to be some type of blood sacrifice made to Him for reasons such as atonement of sin? We are born with this knowledge. Even primitive tribes know this. These facts are the basis for all missionaries to be sent out to bring the truth of Jesus Christ, who is the Blood Covenant, to all peoples.

Did you know that *Jehovah Elohim's* name means "the Covenant-making and Covenant-keeping God"? The One who cuts covenant and ratifies by oath! His name appears more than 50 times in the book of Genesis and over 2,500 times in the Bible.

Did you know there are over 32,000 promises recorded in the Bible? Here's how to receive them: be in covenant, trust, believe, obey, enforce and keep its two greatest commandments. In other words, "You shall love the Lord Your God with all your heart, with all your soul, and with all your mind," and "You shall love your neighbor as yourself."

Did you know that as long as the people of Israel kept covenant they needed no weapons and there was not recorded a single casualty of war?

Do you have any sons or daughters still in Egypt? Covenant will bring them out! It will provide a way of escape not only for you but also for all your household. It will even make all your "Ishmaels" heirs to the kingdom of God!

When you understand covenant, the gospel message will be simple. Your understanding of the Scriptures will all tie in to the big picture, Plan A, God's purpose.

Do not make a covenant with someone you cannot trust. Those of you who might be thinking of marriage, did you hear that? Take time to know the person. Can you really trust that person, his character and his word? Does he/she love you more that himself/herself?

Did you know that every word of God to us is part of the covenant? Heaven and earth will pass away, but His covenant will not pass away and His every Word will be fulfilled! Now that's a promise!

Did you know that utter dependency can be a good thing? That is, if God is your Enabler, and not man. Co-dependency with people is the scheme of the devil so that you're not able to be utterly dependent on *El Shaddai*, the mother-breasted God. God wants to give you milk, honey, meat, bread, water, love and all that He has, but He doesn't want you to have any idol as your source. Spiritual dyslexia is the result of seeing things without the help of the Holy Spirit, who should be your spiritual bifocals. Any family not in Blood Covenant with Elohim through our Lord and Savior Jesus Christ can be classified as dysfunctional!

The New Covenant Governs All Relationships by Love

Jesus summed up the entire Old Covenant in the proper conduct of the following two key relationships found in Matthew 22:36-40:

1. *Love* God with all your being: spirit, soul and body.

2. *Love* your neighbor as yourself.

God, Himself is a triune relationship governed by love. Made in His image and likeness, we are to have dominion by means of the power of love as He has showed us. Relationships in love are a high priority to God. Wrong relationships are the root cause of all the problems we face in this world, such as wars, divorce, abortions, sexual abuse, drug and alcohol abuse, and every other abuse you can name. The principle in effect here is: whenever the product, man, deviates from the design of the Manufacturer, God, he will malfunction. Whenever we step away from these two love commandments of relationship, we will self-destruct in time and need to be returned to the Maker to be fixed. You cannot avoid being in relationships. You're a vital part of this relationship equation. You'll either be a positive part of its solution, or a negative part of its problem.

You have to understand and see that a relationship is a whole unit and is a sum total of all those parts that are involved. It is only as strong as its strongest unit or as weak as its strongest unit. If you are not in covenant with the Almighty, your relationships are only as strong as the strongest person in it. When we are in a love covenant with God, He makes strong our weaknesses. Also, a relationship as a unit is equally as valuable as the total people in it, such as a marriage or family. Jesus came to restore and make right all relationships, not only our relationship with God, but also our relationship with others. By others I mean all people: all races; all strangers; all enemies; all friends; all family members; all parents; all those in authority; all brothers and sisters in Christ! That's why a man or a woman in and of themselves cannot fulfill all the love requirements of the opposite sex.

If you are not in covenant with the Almighty, your relationships are only as strong as the strongest person in it.

How do I know if My Romantic Relationships Are in Order?

"What about *proper romantic relationships*?" you ask. Thanks for asking! These relationships have been devastatingly abused. "What about *proper sexual relationships*?" you further ask. Let's take a look at the order God demands so that our hearts might function properly.

1. First, you need to have a personal relationship with Him. With Him you become a whole single person.

You now have a numerical value of one (1). (This is where I was first off.)

2. Now, as a whole single person with your identity being defined in your relationship with God, you know who you are!

3. Because you know who you are, your mind, will and emotions will mature.

4. Now that you are properly aligned and in order, you, as a whole single person, are qualified to pursue another whole single person for a romantic relationship for the purpose of marriage. One times one = one. Not ½ times ½ = ¹/₄.

The world says: "Go find another person. Try them on for size. If it works, your mind, will and emotions will come to order. You'll be a better person as you find your new identity. Now that you are with the other person, if the other person has problems, you can change them; if you get along O.K. maybe then you can seek God together." *Not!* This is upside down!

There are only two types of romantic relationships we have to consider: *married* and *not married*. Whether they are proper romantic relationships or not has very much to do with the proper sexual relationship plan they will prescribe to: either God's or their own. Let's look at both of these through the eyes of God's Word.

We do agree that love must govern us and our relationships, don't we? Then let's proceed to define our terms so as to fully communicate. The depth of loving is known by the degree of giving and blessing (see Jn. 15:13).

Definition: Love (*Agape*, the highest form) is a choice I make to value a person as God does and to speak and behave in a manner which facilitates the greatest benefit and blessing coming to that person. Or more simply, the desire to *give* to *benefit others* and choose the *highest good* for them! Both *eros* (erotic), a passionate love and *phileo* (brotherly), an affectionate love come from *agape* love and are proper in a covenant marriage. *Agape* love's diametrical opposite is lust. As we have seen, lust is its highly popular alternative in the kingdom of darkness, which selfishly governs it with control, manipulation and fear.

Definition: Lust in its definition desires to *get*, not give, for the *benefit* of *self*, at the *expense* of *others*! We stated earlier in 1 John 2:15-17 that "he who loves the world, the love of the Father is not in him, for all that is in the world—the lust of the flesh, the lust of the eyes, and the pride of life—is not of the Father but is of the world."

We simply now need to put these definitions to the test and place them next to the two romantic relationships and let them determine what is proper or not and what you must choose if you want to do your Father's will.

Unfortunately, the explanations that follow are not going to be fashionable to the contemporary scene. Wrong relationships are the hottest topics today on the TV. They have created a market for numerous talk shows such as Oprah, Dr. Phil, Montel, Rikki, Leeza, Maury, Jerry, etc. & etc. They are mass marketed by many forms of media and seem to be the primary theme of most forms of entertainment. It is a shame that we are being educated and influenced by TV, magazines, books and secular psychologists instead of the Bible. None of these shows mention the "truth" of Jesus Christ as the solution to all of these warped relationships. If they did, they would go off the air. Their ratings would drop because the audience is obsessed with this relationship controversy.

God created sex to be pure, holy, sacred and righteous.

I believe some are looking for answers but don't like the ones God has. The world thinks wrong romantic relationships are the result of "head" problems and don't realize they actually stem from "heart" problems. The topics of broken relationships, divorce, fornication, adultery, and overall oppression will only be dealt with superficially and bandaged up without the "Helper" and "Maker" of our hearts doing the surgery and destroying the "root cause." We walk around spiritually and emotionally wounded and man is attempting to fix himself with carnal ointments.

1. **Sexual Relationship in Marriage**. Again, God created sex to be pure, holy, sacred and righteous. Its purpose was for the reproduction of life within the walled protection of a marriage covenant to insure the maximum blessings for the child. Sexual intercourse is the sign of the celebration of the marriage covenant. It should never come with abuse or force or in anger. It excels when we are unselfish and listening to each other's heart, communicating with sensitivity, with touching, with small talk and with tenderness. (See **Marriage, a Love Covenant** p.79.) Marriage fits neatly into the definition of love by

175

God's design and purpose. "Marriage is honorable among all, and the bed undefiled; but fornicators and adulterers God will judge" (Heb. 13:4).

My friends, that pretty well sums up the parameters of proper sexual relationship according to the inspired Word of God. The only place it was designed to be pure and holy, between one male and one female, is in holy matrimony. Sex, or "eros" love, outside of one's marriage is not pure or holy and not even considered romance, but has defaulted to the definition of lust. Love always benefits the kingdom of God and obeys the Word of the King. Lust never benefits the kingdom of God but makes one become a slave to obey the master he serves. Love always satisfies. Lust never satisfies, but torments. Lust is the torment and emotion of hell that can never be quenched. "To the pure all things are pure, but to those who are defiled and unbelieving nothing is pure; but even their mind and conscience are defiled" (Tit. 1:15).

2. **Sexual Relationship for those not married**. Simple: it is *lust*, not love, according to God's Word. It comes with pain to the heart. *No exceptions to the rule!* It is sin! It violates its covenant purpose. It will not bless but will eventually bring death to the heart, mind, will, and emotions.

Men, your purity, honesty and sexual wholeness are the core of your integrity and you were created for the glory of God. Your integrity is the core of your character. You were designed to cultivate the woman and her heart, not to abuse the creation. You were

176

designed to take care of her as God's daughter, to protect her, honor her and provide an environment for her to flourish. Your words regarding her have the power, both far and near, to bless or curse her heart. Do not degrade womanhood by your words, jokes, or showing off before your friends. Stand above the crowd. Be a leader. Set the standard.

Women, your sexual purity, likewise, is a love gift from God, given to you to be later given for the glory of your husband. It is your glory to be given away only to your husband. Until you marry, this glory is for Jesus, who in turn gives it to the man. Your glory and purity are what make you unique and set apart from all other women. It is not to be given away in any other manner. Anyone can be irresponsible in how they dress so that other eyes would be tempted and lust for what is not theirs to see. Anyone can show cleavage and their navel. Don't cheapen your worth by joining the immoral majority. Have class always. Virginity is the answer to abortion, promiscuity, hurts, perversion, and disease.

Sex and covenant are designed to be sacred, holy and rare, not common. Rare means valuable. Today's culture has perverted our minds. In America, sexual relationships, no matter when, where, or with whom, are viewed as synonymous with love. In reality, they are for the most part its counterfeit, lust, according to God's Word. Sex has been associated with evil rather than glory, purity and holiness. Sleeping together, living together, and conception outside of marriage have become acceptable by the "moral" majority. Huge problem! You have excluded God and His blessings for your prosperity. The very thing needed to improve your relationship, you have shut the door on.

There is a new culture of young people called "True Love Waits" who promise to save themselves for their spouse. They are given purity rings to wear as a symbol of their commitment. This purity ring is to be later given to their spouse at their wedding ceremony.

Sexual intercourse is a spiritual act. It was designed for maximum intimacy, pleasure and procreation. *Ignorance of the purpose of a thing causes experimentation and abuse.* This is true of sex outside of marriage. Experimentation fits the definition of lust. Since sex is the sign of the celebration of the marriage covenant, with regard to adultery, fornication, masturbation, homosexuality, and the like, just what are you celebrating? Certainly not the glory of God or His Kingdom! You are promoting the other kingdom of self and its prince, Satan! See it as it is: sin! The devil derives worship from sexual intercourse outside of marriage. I pray you get the revelation to never tithe again to the enemy. It's nothing but the wrong tree in disguise! Lust promises love but can deliver only torment.

Let's Compare Courtship to Dating

(God's ancient way with today's contemporary counterpart)

Courtship follows the definition of a romantic love relationship. Traditionally, it goes back to the ancient Hebrew culture and was designed to last one year. During this year both parties agreed this time was to be spent for the specific purpose of seeing if they were equally yoked to be married. They met with the parents to obtain their approval and blessing and began a relationship with them also. During this courtship they were not allowed to be alone or without a chaperon.

Also during this period they would pray and seek God to hear from heaven as to whether they were to be wed or not. They were not allowed to get physical at any time or say things that would plant the improper emotional heart seeds. Adultery was punished severely by stoning. The culture knew the consequences for the child conceived out of wedlock. Divorce was almost non-existent and blessings were almost always insured. There are still some countries today that practice courtship. Spain is one example where the young women are accompanied by chaperons and cannot be alone with a young suitor.

Dating today, or going steady with the opposite sex, has been defined as more than a casual friendship. Now it's starting in grade school! I don't understand its popularity, even being tolerated by parents. Parents, toughen up! Dating often now includes sexual intimacy and emotional involvement as part of its overall consideration. Therefore it falls under the definition of lust. It almost always involves sexual intercourse and is a scheme of the devil that is self-managed.

The motive of the male is most often what he can get from the female rather than give. The motive of the female is most often what she can give, but it's not hers to give away. Romantic words that plant seeds into one's heart, such as "I love you," will simply go to seed and grow. Words are spirit and they have power to create and give birth to heart ties. When they are sown outside of marriage, they create bondage, instead of creating bonding in marriage as they were designed.

When a young man tells a woman he loves her and starts this heart process in her, then proceeds to take advantage of those love promises and has sexual intercourse, then does not marry her, or has no intention to ever marry her, he is a fraud. His words are a lie and he can't stand up to the responsibility or accountability of those words that should represent his integrity, name and character. He has defrauded her heart.

Of course, women can also seduce the men with the power they have over sex and with the wrong motives. That is also fraud. The results are broken hearts, bondage and difficulty in breaking the unhealthy tie to cleave to another person. Remember, we must leave to cleave! A person's spirit and soul receive sexual intercourse and foreplay as confirmation and signs of covenant marriage. They become confused when the other person is no longer in the picture and another enters.

We used to call having sex outside of marriage "getting a piece." The promiscuous person then would go about getting a "piece" here and another "piece" there. Now, the spirit and soul are not sure which "piece" is the one they are designed to cleave to. The spiritual and emotional baggage caused by the abuse of your sexuality will be carried into every relationship thereafter. It will accumulate and become a yoke and burden too heavy for you to tote. You will have lost your capacity to give your marriage partner to be all of your love because you have given a piece of your heart out to all those other "pieces". You will have to face the weight of this baggage one day, however, and all baggage carried by your marriage partner. A tough price to pay for the consequences of sexual activity before its time.

When is dating OK? When it is courting.

It's all about the motive of the heart.

Dating and breaking up are actually practice for divorce. The only remedy will come when the revelation of Jesus Christ, His blood, and the power of the Holy Spirit are applied to heal the broken heart and restore its wholeness. Dating is dumb going to seed and becoming a mountain. When is dating OK? When it is courting. It's all about the motive of the heart.

This is a real life dating example from my life.

It all started back in the 60s. I was aware of the attraction gift God put in us for the opposite sex, and I had my share of curiosity toward sex. Like most, I was still innocent through grade school. We had 8th grade parties with records and dancing, but it was harmless for the most part. For lack of knowledge and for lack of a culture that taught us about the schemes of the enemy, I can see, little by little, as I play back my video, how dating came about. It wasn't "cool" to not have kissed a girl by the 8th grade. At one of the parties we each took a turn kissing the girls in the dark. No coincidence that it starts in the dark, to hide. Something about this was very exciting, but not appropriate. I can see my conscience being influenced by my flesh to "shut up" so I could have "fun".

181

High school was a four year progressive lesson in "what I shouldn't have learned from the tree of the 'knowledge of good and evil'." I yielded to the peer pressure that said I must have a "steady girlfriend" to be cool like the upperclassmen. After two hormonal years of hearing and talking about sex, I decided in my junior year to pick a girlfriend who was available. It was honest in the beginning, but not for long. Because to me a "steady date" had the connotation of implied ownership of that person, I started to get very emotionally attached by the exchange of our words. I now was experiencing jealousy even when she would talk to another boy or look at one. We got closer emotionally, and then physically, as time passed by.

One night at the encouragement of a friend, we were going to take our girlfriends to "park" and "make out". At this time parking and making out was just kissing and touching. My spirit and my flesh were arguing the entire time and my flesh prevailed. I felt so ashamed after I had improperly touched her that I couldn't look at her without feeling bad for what I had done to her in violating her innocence. Time went by as we "dated" and experimented more with our sexuality. I wanted to have intercourse with her but it never happened because she was trying to remain a virgin. Nevertheless, in the soul and spiritual realm the damage was already done to her heart when I decided to leave her.

When I broke off the relationship, it almost killed her. She was a wonderful person but my selfish motives of getting sex and pleasure at her expense and then breaking it off severely hurt her. Furthermore, my sexual desires had been released prematurely and I began looking for the next sexual relationship. Thus began a course that I had set for myself and could not ever seem to escape or satisfy.

See, lust never satisfies but torments. I left behind a trail of broken hearts and hurts due to my pride, selfishness, and lust. And to think it started out with the simple thought and question of what's wrong with "dating"? This stronghold of thinking was going to continue to take a terrible toll on my future relationships, marriage and children. I couldn't stop it!

One day, over twenty years later, I bumped into this same girl I dated in high school. Earlier, we had coincidentally run into each other a few times, but this was to be the day I was going to hear from her heart. I noticed her and her mother sitting in a booth at a pizzeria. My wife and I sat down in the booth with them to say hello. An unpleasant and most revealing conversation ensued.

She said that she had loved me and was trying so hard to be a "good girl" for God and me. Since she didn't "put out" sexually, she believed that I had left her for someone who would. She couldn't eat for days and had an emotional breakdown. Her mother, in her mind, already had the two of us married and she told others the same. Because of my words and their power, and according to my actions, I had defrauded this woman in her heart. She said that I had ruined her life (which really meant destroyed her heart).

Her mother said I had "stood her up" for prom and left her without a date, ruining her entire senior year and high school experience. I didn't ask her to the prom but asked another girl the middle of senior year. It wasn't true that I stood her up, but to her heart, which was already married to me, it was.

I told her I was sorry, but that didn't help one bit twenty years later. She said her life had never recovered from that experience. Her countenance and the pain in her expression clearly showed it was true. The damage was immeasurable.

Now only Jesus can help her. She is a victim and a statistic like a multitude of others that have been devastated by the culturally acceptable practice of dating. She even had a problem with God, because she thought that through her obedience to Him, she lost me.

Men, when we act in this manner we give the wrong image of God and men and all those in authority! This woman now thinks all men will hurt her. She later failed in her first marriage and I don't know if she ever remarried. Both she and the next man in her life have to deal with all the baggage and damage that has accumulated.

Heavenly Father, I pray for her and I ask your forgiveness. I repent and ask forgiveness to all the women I have hurt and all the women who read this and have been hurt by men this way. On behalf of all men, women, I ask your forgiveness! We have sinned against you! We have hurt your precious hearts and have stolen your glory. Holy Spirit, I ask Your help to heal their broken hearts in the name of Jesus! Where they have been hurt and have felt cursed, Father, I ask you to bless Your daughters' hearts. Help them, Holy Spirit, to forgive us, so they will be set free from the bitterness we have caused. Renew in them a clean heart, oh God, and restore a right spirit within them! Jesus, thank you for forgiving our sins and for healing them. Wash them with Your blood, Jesus, and make them feel as white as snow. Thank You, Jesus, for paying the price with Your Life for all the hearts we have damaged!

The New Covenant

Principles of Covenant Life

(to be discussed in home groups for practical application)

1. Commitment and covenant are like love and marriage: you can't have one without the other! If you don't have commitment, you are not in covenant. You've left out your heart from the engagement.

2. Salvation begins with Jesus on your lips, but is not consummated until His Covenant nature is in your heart! When you first ask Him into your heart, the process begins. It is not finished until He is Lord of All your heart.

3. Salvation is like when you first sign to purchase a home. The home is not yours until you go to the closing <u>table</u>. Blood Covenant is the deal closed!

4. Faith is the title deed to your house, that contains rights as a citizen under the Covenant to His subdivision, called the Kingdom of God.

5. You will fully benefit from covenant when you understand that by faith and grace Jesus has made you 100% righteous.

6. By receiving the New Covenant, Jesus, you receive "*sozo*" the Greek word for salvation. *Sozo* is the whole covenant package. It includes: rebirth, redemption, sanctification, justification, salvation, and RIGHTEOUSNESS!

7. Until you are baptized with water and the Holy Spirit, you cannot see or enter the Kingdom of God (John 3:3-5).

8. Jesus is the Door. (John 10:1-9). If any one enters by Him, He will be saved. He is the Threshold Covenant. His blood is at the door.

9. In the beginning was the Covenant, and the Covenant was with God, and the Covenant was God. And the Covenant became flesh and dwelt among us. Jesus is the New Covenant.

10. The power and life of the King were in the blood of Jesus! Everything that was unrighteous about you was changed by this holy, precious blood of the Lamb.

11. Jesus knew the price He had to pay on the cross at Calvary before He said, "Let Us make man." Now that's love!

12. How do you feel when you realize that Jesus is in you, and you are in Him sitting on His throne at the right hand of God the Father? WOWOWOWOW!

Questions for Further Thought

1. Have you entered the Blood Covenant with Jesus by accepting Him as your Savior? _____ If not, are you ready to make that decision? Don't wait. Do it now.

   _____

   If you have accepted Jesus as your Savior, do you also acknowledge Him as Lord of your life, giving Him complete control? _____ If not, do it now.

2. How does it make you feel to know that the blood of Jesus has made you *righteous*?_____

   _____

   _____

The New Covenant

Prayer of Exchange

(Say this prayer out loud and ask the
Holy Spirit to help you receive its truth.)

Jesus, I thank You for giving Your life for me, so
here is what I exchange on my part at the cross:

Dear Lord, my life is Yours. All that I have and all
that I am are Yours. My past, present, future and
time are Yours. My talent is Yours, my eyes are
Yours, my tongue is Yours, my thoughts are Yours
and my sexuality is Yours. My testimony is Yours,
my will is Yours, my work is Yours, my walk is
Yours and my worship is Yours. My children are
Yours. All my heart, all my soul, all my mind and all
possessions of value I lay at Your feet as my gifts to
You. All my flesh, self, sins, and all weapons I also
give to You. I freely and gladly relinquish all of these
at the foot of Your cross to be sacrificed on Your
altar on Your cross with You.

Jesus, I receive Your words in response to me that
renew my identity as You say, "All *I AM.......* *the Bread
of Life, The Light of the world, The Door of the sheep,
The Good Shepherd, the Resurrection and the Life, the
True and Living Way, and the True Vine* and all that
I have are now yours, including My eternal life. My
kingdom is yours; you are now My son/daughter and
joint heir with Me. My righteousness is yours and
now you are cleansed with My blood. You are in me,
the Savior, who is the Omnipotent, Omnipresent,
Almighty, Triune, Eternal God. You are now bone of

My bone and flesh of My flesh and branches of Me, the Vine. I give to you all My Love, all My grace and all My blessings. You will be complete in Me and your walk will be fruitful. You can now stand fearless in the face of Satan, the counterfeit lion, because you are in Me, the true Lion of the tribe of Judah. Heaven is open to you 24 hours a day and forever. All the authority in heaven and earth are yours; all of heaven's ability, glory, and strength are at your disposal and request, My covenant-keeping child. I give you My spear, yes the spear of the Chief in exchange for your goat. I give you *My Name* and *My Personality:*

1. Jehovah YAHWEH, I Am what I Am, I will be who I will be. (Exodus 3:14-16)

2. Jehovah Elohim, the Lord, your Creator. (Genesis 2:4)

3. Jehovah El Elyon, the Lord, the Most High God, your Owner. (Genesis 14:22)

4. Jehovah Adonai, the Lord, your Master. (Genesis 15:2)

5. Jehovah El Olam, the Lord, the Everlasting. (Genesis 21:23)

6. Jehovah Jireh, the Lord your Provider. (Genesis 22:14)

7. Jehovah Rapha, the Lord, your Healer. (Exodus 15:26)

8. Jehovah Nissi, the Lord, your Banner. (Exodus 17:15)

9. Jehovah Makaddesh Kem, the Lord your Sanctification. (Exodus 31:13)

10. Jehovah Shalom, the Lord your Peace. (Judges 6:24)

11. Jehovah Shaphat, the Lord your Judge. (Judges 11:27)

12. Jehovah Saboath, the Lord of Hosts. (1 Samuel 1:3)

13. Jehovah Zidkenu, the Lord your Righteousness. (Jeremiah 23:6)

14. Jehovah Raah, the Lord your Shepherd. (Psalm 23:1)

15. Jehovah Elyon, the Lord your Blesser. (Psalm 7:17)

16. Jehovah Hosenu, the Lord your Maker. (Psalms 95:6)

17. Jehovah Gibbor, the Lord the Mighty. (Isaiah 42:13)

18. Jah -Jehovah, the Lord your Jehovah. (Isaiah 12:2; 26:4)

19. Jehovah Shammah, the Lord the Everpresent. (Ezekiel 48:35)

20. Jehovah Jehoshua Mashiach, the Lord Jesus Christ. (Matthew 1:21; Acts 2:36)

These are all part of your new name and identity. I give you legal right and "power of attorney" to use My name; I even give you My engagement ring, My Promise, My Holy Spirit. He'll write My laws on your heart. He will be your Helper and Comforter in union of being with Me and My Father. He will circumcise the flesh from your heart and as you submit to Me, He will submit to you. He will prepare you as My living word and My living epistle and you will not return to Me void or empty. You will abide in Me and I in you and I will be with you always. I will be coming back for you for our Wedding Feast. Prepare yourself!"

Lord, I receive these words. Holy Spirit, plant them deep into my heart and bring them always to my remembrance. The enemy will not steal these words from me; they are sealed with the blood of Jesus! Amen.

Chapter 8

Returning to Eden

※◈◈◈※

D id you pray that last prayer of exchange? You need
to. Let it penetrate your heart. When I first heard
and then received and then believed this covenant
revelation of all Jesus did for me because He loved me, my
heart renewal process ignited. With that knowledge, all so
wonderful, came understanding and so my new heart's
foundation was established. My heart's questioning was
over. My New Covenant in Jesus redefined, redirected,
reconstructed, reconciled, redeemed and restored me. Now
I know who I am, where I am going, what my purpose is,
what potential I have, and who my source is. They were all
found in one word: *Jesus!*

Now it was time to build my house on that Rock with
Wisdom Himself. I literally started my life again as a
"brand new creation" because I now had the heart of Jesus
in me. I could see and hear from the eyes and mind of

Christ in me. Now that I was a whole person for the first time, I qualified as a covenant initiator for a marriage relationship. And so Jill and I, both with covenant understanding and a new belief system, proceeded to the altar.

Don't get me wrong, Jill still had her doubts. Remember, we were divorced for two years, and had a rocky ten years before that. Could she ever trust me with heart again? This wasn't going to be an automatic, instantaneous, believing for a miracle, fool-proof endeavor. It was still subject to applying all this truth to our new life together. Is this available to all who have been divorced? No. It will only work for two parties in agreement to lay down their lives for each other and in submission to Jesus. We had to enter into this new marriage by faith and trust in God and trusting each other to walk in God's ways. Was it going to be different from the past on the other side of the ceremony? Yes!

Oh, the marriage ceremony! It was performed on earth but all of heaven came down and joined in. It was a place, a spot, a moment, a presence, a door...Does this sound familiar? Angels attended the electrifying atmosphere while the extraordinary, anointed music filled the sanctuary. Pastor Craig Hill was ready; I was ready. Jill's entire body kept shaking. Her heart was on the line. She was about to enter into a realm into which she had never gone before, with the commitment that once she did, she couldn't ever leave again. We all sensed we were in all reality standing before God on holy ground. We had returned to Eden. Before God, a host of angels, and over one hundred witnesses, we crossed over a threshold and exchanged our covenant vows after laying down and relinquishing our weapons, rights and possessions. Our vows in essence were, "All I am and all I have are yours, and I would rather die than break my commitment to love you second only to Jesus Christ." We dedicated our marriage that day to the Holy Spirit which, incidentally, was the greatest decision, next to receiving Jesus as Lord and Savior, and our lives from that moment forward have been changed dramatically.

I went from a marriage basher to a marriage counselor. Imagine such a turn around! I truly regret hurting all those people while I was learning how to do it God's way. I hope they can find it in their hearts to forgive me with the help of Jesus. Now my covenant partner and I have become marriage ministers and pastors of a church. It has been quite an adventurous fifteen years since our covenant marriage. However, God has been faithful.

I suffered a stroke in 1992. I couldn't speak or even say my name, yet I walked out of the hospital three days later resurrected and healed. I couldn't work, couldn't talk and had no insurance, but more than $10,000 in hospital bills were canceled. God proved faithful. I have had more than thirty kidney stones in my life, one on my wedding day that dissolved by prayer before the ceremony, and I have been healed of stones. God proved faithful. Our son, Angelo, jumped off a cliff one hundred feet high and landed short of the water hole he was aiming for. He landed on his head and shoulder and was knocked unconscious. At the hospital the x-rays showed a broken clavicle and collapsed lung, yet Angelo walked out of the hospital the next day with subsequent x-rays showing no sign of anything but healing. God is faithful.

God sent us as ministers to a town of 2000 in the plains of western Kansas. We had no money, no job; only enough for a one-way U-Haul load of stuff. It was a total culture shock for us after the colorful Colorado Rockies and the Denver metro area with over a million people. The people in the town didn't want us there. We were a threat to the traditional religious folk. But we survived! God trained us there in that classroom of experience. Again, He proved faithful.

We carried a mandate to re-establish God's covenant principles in this U.S.A. heartland state. Four years later we moved to Hays, Kansas, where we now reside and where we bought a bar and converted it into a community church and business. Do you think that seems odd? After all, God took me out of the bars and brought me to church. With God nothing is impossible. We are teaching God's people covenant principles. Marriages are being restored, families are being put back in order and lost individuals are becoming covenant citizens of the kingdom of God. Not by might, not by our power, but "by My Spirit," says the Lord. Without a single day's lack He has provided our finances, our health and our housing. God keeps His promises. After fifteen covenant years Jill and I are still on our perpetual honeymoon and our love continues to grow with time. But, that's another book.

My friend, as we approach our final destination, we will be arriving back at the beginning. Just as it took Moses 40 years to journey in a circle to a location not far from his first departure, so we too are returning to Eden 6000 years later, the place where we first fell. The difference this time, however, is that we have eaten of the "tree of life," Jesus Christ! Eden, as we said, means a spot or place where we find the presence of God. Because we now are in the New Covenant, Jesus Christ, everywhere He goes, we go also. In reality, since we have eaten freely from "the tree of life," the blessed fruit is in us and we in Him. If you are in the New Covenant and its intimate fellowship, everywhere the presence of Jesus is can be called Eden.

Because we now are in the New Covenant, Jesus Christ, everywhere He goes, we go also.

Let's go to the book of Revelation to see some of the events that are to take place for us as His covenant partners. This romance never ends!

Here are some of His promises to us, all in covenant language.

> *"I am the Alpha and the Omega, the Beginning and the End," says the Lord, "who is and who was and who is to come, the Almighty"* (Revelation 1:8).

And as He said to the apostle John, He says to us,

> *Do not be afraid; I am the First and the Last. I am He who lives, and was dead, and behold, I am alive forevermore. Amen. And I have the keys of Hades and of Death* (Revelation 1:17-18).

> *He who has an ear, let him hear what the Spirit says to the churches. To him who overcomes I will give to eat from the tree of life, which is in the midst of the Paradise of God* (Revelation 2:7).

> *Be faithful until death, and I will give you the crown of life* (the crown as a son of the King). *He who has*

195

an ear, let him hear what the Spirit says to the churches. He who overcomes shall not be hurt by the second death (Revelation 2:10-11).

He who has an ear, let him hear what the Spirit says to the churches. To him who <u>overcomes</u> I will give some of the hidden manna to eat (the body of Jesus, the Bread of Life). *And I will give to him a white stone, and on the stone a new name written* (your new married name to the King which confirms your real identity) *which no one knows except him who receives it* (Revelation 2:17).

But hold fast what you have till I come. And he who overcomes, and keeps My works until the end, to him I will give power over the nations—...as I also have received from My Father; and I will give him the morning star. He who has an ear, let him hear what the Spirit says to the churches (Revelation 2:25-29).

He who overcomes shall be clothed in white garments, and I will not blot out his name from the Book of Life; but I will confess his name before My Father and before His angels. He who has an ear, let him hear what the Spirit says to the churches (Revelation 3:5-6).

Because you have kept My command to persevere, I also will keep you from the hour of trial which shall come upon the whole world (but we are no longer of the world), *to test those who dwell on the earth...He who overcomes, I will make him a pillar in the temple of My God, and he shall go out no more* (as will we as did David when Saul took him in). *I will write on him the name of My God and the name of the city of My God, the New Jerusalem, which comes down from heaven from My God. And I will write on him My new name.* (the King of kings, and the Lord of lords) *He who has an ear, let him hear what the Spirit says to the churches* (Revelation 3:10-13).

Behold, I stand at the door and knock. If any one hears My voice and opens the door, I will come in to him and dine with him, and he with Me. (Threshold Covenant!) *To him who <u>overcomes</u> I will grant to sit with Me on My throne, as I also overcame and sat down with My Father on His throne. He who has an ear, let him hear what the Spirit says to the churches* (Revelation 3:20-22).

What a tremendous Word! Thanks to what happened at Pentecost, as Jesus had promised to give us His Holy Spirit, we too received His baptism and the sign of the New Covenant, a reborn spirit. Now we have an ear to hear what the Spirit is saying. How do we overcome?

And they overcame him by the blood of the Lamb and the word of their testimony, and they did not love their lives to the death (Revelation 12:11).

In other words, we overcome by the blood of our Covenant partner! Hallelujah! This Covenant relationship *is* our testimony! The devil no longer has dominion over us, but we have dominion over him!

John saw God on His throne in heaven, and He appeared like a jasper and sardius stone, and what else but the covenant sign, a rainbow around the throne, in appearance like an emerald (see Rev. 4:3). He saw a scroll in God's right hand and one of the elders said to John,

> *"Do not weep. Behold, the Lion of the tribe of Judah, the Root (seed) of David, has prevailed to open the scroll and to loose its seven seals"* (Revelation 5:5).

John saw the Lamb (Jesus), take the scroll and the creatures and elders said to Him:

> *"You are worthy to take the scroll, and to open its seals; For You were slain, and have redeemed us to God by Your Blood out of every tribe and tongue and people and nation, and have made us kings and priests to our God; And we shall reign on the earth"* (Revelation 5:9-10).

Yes, Jesus paid the price and bought us back to God and reconciled us with our Father. At last we will reign and have dominion as He first said when He created us.

Later, John heard the *seventh trumpet* as it sounded and the voices in heaven were saying:

> *"The kingdoms of this world have become the kingdoms of our Lord and of His Christ, and He shall reign forever and ever!" And the twenty-four elders who sat before God on their thrones fell on their faces and worshiped God, saying: "We give You thanks, O Lord God Almighty, the One who is and who was and who is to come, because You have taken Your great power and reigned. The nations were angry, and Your wrath has come, and the time of the dead, that they should be judged, and that You should reward Your servants the prophets and*

the saints, and those who fear Your name, small and great, and should destroy those who destroy the earth." Then the temple of God was opened in heaven, and the ark of His covenant was seen in His temple. And there were lightnings, noises, thunderings, an earthquake, and great hail (Revelation 11:15-19).

Haven't you seen this demonstration before? We serve a dramatic, demonstrative, powerful Covenant God!

Can you see now to what length God will go to see that His Word performs that which it was sent to do? Revelation 13:8 makes reference to the "Lamb that was slain from the foundation of the world." For God so loved us, that before He agreed to "Let us make man...," He knew what sacrifice this Covenant Word demanded to be fully carried out. How awesome is His love! How profound is His Word! It is "who He is"! It is who you are! It contains your potential and destiny! Should we know it, read it, taste it, eat it, drink from it, meditate upon it? With every fiber and breath of our being we should! All of creation came into being through this Word. From Genesis 1 to Revelation 22, this Word exploded and became manifest to us. What a plan! What precision! What design! What orchestration! What order! What Love! Off the charts! Beyond quantum mathematics! Beyond our limited comprehension is the plan of our Father, Lord, and King!

The Marriage Supper of the Lamb

Are you starting to understand the overall macrocosm of the Bible as a covenant relationship between God and man? Our marriages were designed to be small pictures or microcosms of this overall love affair. The apostle John heard the announcement of our coming great covenant wedding celebration as he wrote:

"Let us be glad and rejoice and give Him glory, for the marriage of the Lamb has come, and His wife has made herself ready." And to her it was granted to be arrayed in fine linen, clean and bright, for the fine linen is the righteous acts of the saints. Then he said to me, "Write: 'Blessed are those who are called to the marriage supper of the Lamb!'" And he said to me, "These are the true sayings of God" (Revelation 19:7-9).

Your Blood Covenant partner has made you worthy to sit at His table!

The Second Coming of Christ

Then John saw heaven opened,

and behold, a white horse. And He who sat on him was called Faithful and True, and in righteousness He judges and makes war. His eyes were like a flame of fire, and on His head were many crowns. He had a name written that no one knew except Himself. He was clothed with a robe dipped in blood, and His name is called The Word of God. And the armies in heaven, clothed in fine linen, white and clean, followed Him on white horses. Now out of His mouth goes a sharp sword, that with it He should strike the nations. And He Himself will rule them with a rod of iron. He Himself treads the winepress of the fierceness and wrath of Almighty God. And He

has on His robe and on His thigh a name written:
KING OF KINGS AND LORD OF LORDS (Revelation
19:11-16).

The Millennial Reign of Christ

John then saw an angel coming down from heaven to
bind Satan for a thousand years, and cast him into the
bottomless pit. He then saw thrones where they sat for
judgment. He said,

> *And I saw thrones, and they sat on them, and judg-*
> *ment was committed to them. Then I saw the souls*
> *of those who had been beheaded for their witness to*
> *Jesus and for the word of God, who had not wor-*
> *shiped the beast or his image, and had not received*
> *his mark on their foreheads or on their hands. And*
> *they lived and reigned with Christ for a thousand*
> *years. But the rest of the dead did not live again until*
> *the thousand years were finished. This is the first*
> *resurrection. Blessed and holy is he who has part in*
> *the first resurrection. Over such the second death*
> *has no power, but they shall be priests of God and of*
> *Christ, and shall reign with Him a thousand years*
> (Revelation 20:4-6).

That's us! This is the reference to all those who overcame
by the blood of the Lamb and the word of their testimony.
This is for all those in Blood Covenant with Jesus. I believe
during this millennium we will continue discipling all nations
in all things pertaining to the New Covenant, Jesus Christ.

The New Heaven, The New Earth, The New Jerusalem

Now I saw a new heaven and a new earth, for the first heaven and the first earth had passed away. Also there was no more sea. Then I, John, saw the holy city, New Jerusalem, coming down out of heaven from God, prepared as a bride adorned for her husband (Revelation 21:1-2).

We're not going up to heaven my brothers and sisters; the New Jerusalem is coming down from the New Heaven and we the kings of the New Earth will bring our glory into it. God will still be the King of heaven and earth and we will be the kings under His authority on earth as it is in heaven. We are sons of the Father and the bride of Jesus Christ, our husband, forevermore. This is in the same fashion that God took Eve from the side of Adam and brought her to him. All those in Covenant in Jesus will be taken by God from within Him to be bone of Jesus' bone, married forever. The New Jerusalem seems to be the eternal honeymoon site!

And I heard a loud voice from heaven saying, "Behold, the tabernacle of God is with men, and He will dwell with them, and they shall be His people. God Himself will be with them and be their God (Revelation 21:3).

THIS IS THE RETURN TO EDEN! All those in Covenant and have overcome "shall inherit all things, and I will be his God and he shall be My son" (Rev. 21:7).

ALL THAT HE HAS AND ALL THAT HE IS, IS OURS! WE NOW ARE THE IMAGE AND LIKENESS OF THE KING AND HAVE DOMINION OVER ALL THINGS, AS HE FIRST SPOKE!

Yes, the New Jerusalem seems to be the bridge between the New Heaven and the New Earth where we have a continuous spiritual connection with God. Of course, views differ somewhat as to its precise explanation. My revelation of this is limited and still in progress until the appointed time. Besides, there is nothing to argue here that won't be revealed as the Holy Spirit wills. All I know is that we will be there to experience it first hand.

A pure river of the water of life proceeds from the throne of God and the Lamb in the New city of Jerusalem and in the middle of its street, and on either side of the river, was the tree of life...it seems that Jesus is everywhere! There will be no more curse. We shall see His face and His name will be on our foreheads, as the blood on the doorposts and lintel, as those marked and whose hearts have been circumcised in covenant. We shall reign forevermore.

"And behold, I am coming quickly, and My reward is with Me, to give to every one according to his work. I am the Alpha and the Omega, the Beginning and the End, the First and the Last"...And the Spirit and the bride say, "Come!" And let him who hears say, Come!"

203

And let him who thirsts come. Whoever desires, let him take the water of life freely (Revelation 22:12-13, 17).

EVEN SO, COME, LORD JESUS! ALL GLORY IS YOURS! AMEN!

Prayer

(Say this prayer out loud, or your own as the
Holy Spirit leads you)

Holy Spirit, I thank You for revealing my Father, my Jesus, and Yourself, my Teacher! Thank You for choosing me before the foundations of the earth to reveal Your awesome purpose and destiny for mankind. I cannot contain all the wonder You have filled me with through Your Living Word! This has been manna from heaven and life to my being.

Lord, I am not worthy in and of myself to receive all of Your blessings. But thank You, Jesus, for Your righteousness, for You are worthy, and You have made me worthy as Your Blood Covenant partner. You are beautiful beyond description, too marvelous for words!

Jesus, I am looking forward to all of the events You have planned for me throughout eternity. I bow my knees and my tongue confesses that You, Jesus Christ are Lord, my Lord and King! I choose to eat of You, the tree of life, and to be holy, set apart, dedicated to You alone, my Savior and Master forever and ever! You alone are my God and I am your son, Father! Your will forever will be mine!

204

I thank you for this journey back to Eden to be forever in Your love and presence. Until You come again, may I be a light and an ambassador on behalf of You, my King. I give You all I am, and all I have, and especially I give You all my heart. I Love You! Amen.

The Beginning!

About the Author

❧❀❧

Robert Scheck and his wife Jill are the founders and senior pastors of Hallelujah Ministries International, located in Hays, Kansas. Their vision is to establish God's covenant principles in the "heartland" of America—dealing with the "issues of the heart" in men, women, and children who cope with divorce, hurting marriages, and rocky relationships. The Scheck's have "been there and done that" when it comes to dealing with the issues of a blended family and broken relationships; now they mentor others on how to minister to the heart and renew marriage vows. Robert and Jill have been married for 25 years.